COLD CASE
MICHIGAN

TOBIN T. BUHK

THE
History
PRESS

Published by The History Press
Charleston, SC
www.historypress.com

First published 2021

Manufactured in the United States

ISBN 9781467148733

Library of Congress Control Number: 2021941627

Notice: The information in this book is true and complete to the best of our knowledge. It is offered without guarantee on the part of the author or The History Press. The author and The History Press disclaim all liability in connection with the use of this book.

Contents

Everyone Likes a Whodunit…A Brief Introduction to
Cold Case Michigan   5

1. The "Spiked Club Triple Murder" (Dowagiac, 1921)   9
2. The Ferndale Head Case (Ferndale, 1927)   22
3. The Doctor, His Wife and the Other Woman (Detroit, 1927)   35
4. The St. Aubin Avenue House of Horrors (Detroit, 1929)   55
5. He Talked Too Much: Jerry Buckley (Detroit, 1930)   78
6. "A Riddle, Wrapped in a Mystery, inside an Enigma"
   (Grand Rapids, 1938)   98
7. The Usual Suspects: The Slaying of Senator Warren Hooper
   (Lansing, 1945)   115
8. The Riddle of Lydia Thompson (Detroit, 1945)   127
9. The Four (Lansing, 1970–1972)   149

For Additional Research   155
About the Author   159

Everyone Likes a Whodunit...

A Brief Introduction to *Cold Case Michigan*

My fatal attraction to historic cold cases began one sunny July day at Heathrow Airport, where I discovered Jack the Ripper.

That summer, my brother and I backpacked across Europe. On the British Airways flight to London, we watched what seemed like a never-ending newsreel of cricket highlights. Despite the five hours of watching cricketers in action, I did not, do not and probably never will understand the game of cricket.

While in Heathrow awaiting the return flight, I faced a choice: watch five more hours of cricket highlights or find another way to pass the time. So I wandered into a shop and began perusing books. That's when I spotted Donald Rumbelow's *The Complete Jack the Ripper*.

It was love at first fright. Over three decades have passed from that fateful moment when I became an amateur Ripperologist and an aficionado of historic true crime.

Jack never visited the Great Lake State (that I know of), but that doesn't mean that Michigan does not have its share of notable unsolved crimes, including Ripperesque murders, the slaughter of entire families, closed-room murders and even a headhunter on the loose.

So why, might the skeptical reader ask, should I pay attention to old, cold cases?

I offer three reasons. One: because identifiable patterns of human behavior exist and have led to profiles compiled over the years, such cases can prove instructive to the student of criminal behavior. Two: if nothing else, they serve as morbid reminders that those ignorant of history will be condemned to repeat it. Three: no matter how much water has flowed under the bridge, the victims of unsolved crimes deserve justice, even if belated by a century, and there is no statute of limitations on murder. Perhaps something between these covers will remind a reader of that suspicious letter found in a trunk in the attic—a letter that contains some clue that may lead to the closure of a centuries-old cold case.

Back to Jack the Ripper. Over 130 years later, the case still lingers in books churned out annually by scores of so-called Ripperologists. Students of the case revisit crime scenes, weigh the evidence and debate suspects all because of the possibility that someday, even after all this time, someone will find the knife and the hand that used it.

Inevitably, with a book like this, some readers will wonder about some famous unsolved cases that did not make the cut. "Yes," they might ask, "but what about…?"

There are literally hundreds of cold cases in Michigan history, enough to fill several volumes. Alas, I had to make some tough decisions about which ones to include. To select the best stories for inclusion, I followed a few simple guidelines:

The crimes had to be headline cases in their respective eras and not obscure matters or minor footnotes in the annals of crime in the Great Lake State. Such footnotes always make interesting reading but do not qualify as the "most infamous unsolved crimes in Michigan history." They also tended to elude the historical record, making verification of facts difficult if not impossible.

The cases had to be verifiable crimes and not the product of suspicion, folklore, rumor or gossip, although all four of these ingredients are required in cooking up a really good cold case story.

The crime could not be written about so much that it became the yesterday's news of yesterday's news, which brings me back to "Yes, but what about…?" The Hoffa case, for example, ranks at the top of unsolved Michigan crimes, yet whole libraries on the case exist.

Alas, the reader will not find Jimmy Hoffa buried in these pages. Instead, the reader will find the slaughter of a family, a headhunter's relics, a closed-room murder, the slaughter of another family, an assassination, a murder without motive or suspects, another assassination and other crimes that will strain the "little grey cells," to borrow an expression from Hercule Poirot.

Each old cold case is like a nonfiction game of *Clue*. Between these covers, readers will find the weapons, the rooms and the suspects, but in this game, the envelope containing the solution remains sealed, the solutions obscured by bungled investigations, crafty criminals who excelled at covering their tracks and the passage of time.

Let the games begin!

1

The "Spiked Club Triple Murder"

(Dowagiac, 1921)

The Monroe family—William and Mary and their two daughters, Neva and Ardith—lived in a small, lean-to shack on a quiet street in Silver Creek Township at the northwest edge of Dowagiac. On the afternoon of Tuesday, September 20, 1921, an eight-year-old neighbor calling on Ardith Monroe stumbled upon one of the grisliest crimes in the history of Southwest Michigan. "It has no parallel in Cass county and perhaps there is none in Michigan," wrote a reporter for the *Dowagiac Daily News* in his page-one item of Thursday, September 22, 1921.

Grace McKee stood on the front porch and called for Ardith Monroe. The eight-year-old wanted to see if her friend, the younger of the two Monroe daughters, could come out to play. When no one answered, she rapped on the door a few times. Still no answer, but it seemed like the family was home, so Grace gingerly opened the front door and went inside. The floorboards creaked under her feet as she tiptoed into the bedroom. As the sun began to drop below the horizon, the last rays of daylight spilled into the room from the gaps around the drawn window shades. The large room contained two steel beds, one shared by husband and wife, the other by the sisters.

When her eyes adjusted to the darkness, Grace noticed Ardith sitting in the corner with her back pressed against the bedroom wall. Her face was

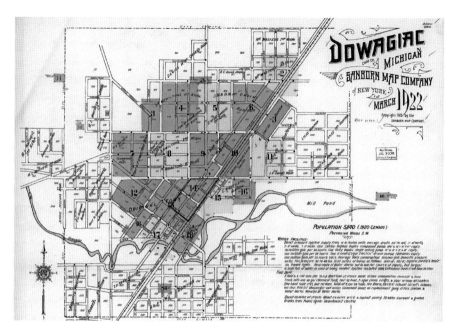

Sanborn Fire Insurance Map showing Dowagiac in 1922. *Library of Congress Geography and Map Division.*

the color of a porcelain doll. A streak of dried blood ran from a gash on her temple just below the hairline down the right side of her face. She stared at the bed and did not appear to notice when her friend entered the room.

Grace McKee followed Ardith's gaze and saw a motionless silhouette stretched across the bed. She let out a yelp and darted out of the house, screaming.

Grace sprinted home. Her mother managed to decipher the jumbled mass of adjectives and called Mary Monroe's brother Ralph Gillette, who immediately went to investigate. Meanwhile, neighbors who heard Grace's screams also called the police. Gillette and a small contingent of neighbors arrived just before the police, and in handling several vital pieces of evidence, they inadvertently tainted the crime scene.

When Officer James Pinnette and County Coroner S.E. Bryant arrived at the Monroe house just minutes later, Pinnette found Ardith lying in a fetal position on the floorboards. Barely conscious, the girl had lost a great deal of blood from the gash in her temple. The killer or killers had apparently clubbed her in the side of the head and left her to bleed out on the floor.

Pinnette lifted Ardith and held her tightly while Bryant examined the scene. The coroner had never seen anything like it. The body of the elder

Monroe daughter—seventeen-year-old Neva—was lying on top of blood-saturated bed linen, tangles of hair spilling over a face pulverized by a mace-like blunt instrument.

The carnage continued in the bed occupied by Neva's parents.

Forty-eight-year-old William Monroe and his forty-two-year-old wife, Mary, lay across the bed, their faces erased by repeated blows with a metal-studded club. The weapon had crushed their cheekbones and flattened their noses, reducing their faces to unrecognizable, pulpy masses of shredded flesh. Thick, syrupy coagulated blood saturated the bedspread, and cast-off stains left the walls covered with crimson specks. The crime had been an incredibly brutal one, yet nothing—no overturned chairs, no smashed lamps, no picture frames hanging askew—appeared to suggest a violent confrontation.

Coroner Bryant concluded that the slayer or slayers climbed through a half-open kitchen window and tiptoed into the bedroom while the Monroe family slept. The perpetrator knocked out each one of them with a succession of single blows and then proceeded to batter them in a frenzied barrage.

Combing the house for clues, a team of investigators made some provocative discoveries. Spoiling groceries on the kitchen table—withering produce and rancid meat—hinted that the murders occurred sometime shortly after Mary Monroe returned from shopping Saturday evening.

Torn pillowcases hinted at the possibility that someone rifled through them looking for Monroe's fabled stash of greenbacks. According to neighborhood lore, William Monroe had been saving to buy a more substantial house but did not keep his money in the bank. Neighbors apparently believed he kept his money secreted somewhere on the property, perhaps in a pillowcase or mattress. Conversely, the pillowcases may have been damaged when the killer repeatedly brought the weapon down on his slumbering victims.

On the floorboards against one of the walls, the killer left the murder weapon: a blood-soaked section of two-by-four with nails protruding from it. Bits of flesh and small clumps of hair were glued to the nails with coagulated blood.

The length of the handmade club matched a piece of wood missing from a lean-to attached to the house outside of the kitchen. The strength needed to wrench the rail away from the structure suggested a big, strong perpetrator. This choice of weapon also suggested a lack of premeditation. Whoever murdered the Monroe family did not bring a pre-fashioned mace to the scene.

The most promising clue came in the form of bloody fingerprints on the two-by-four. A fingerprint expert made impressions of the marks, which detectives hoped would link the murder weapon to the murderer, but the effort proved futile. The number of people who had traipsed through the crime scene destroyed any evidentiary value of the club, the clothes worn by the victims and things the killer likely touched as he entered and exited the cottage, such as door frames and window sashes. Of all the possible clues the cottage potentially contained, detectives managed to lift one single fingerprint from the club, and it was of questionable value to the investigation.

The Monroe residence made the ideal location for the perpetrator to slip into and out of unseen. The house stood at the end of the street, approximately one hundred yards from the nearest neighbor. The police theorized that the perpetrator could have hid behind the house, waiting for an opportune moment, and then crawled through one of the windows without notice. At one hundred yards distant, the neighbors might hear a struggle, but the crime scene suggested that no such scuffle had occurred.

According to the headline story about the macabre discovery in the *Dowagiac Daily News*, Pinnette attempted to question Ardith on the spot. "Girlie, do you know who did this?"

Traumatized, Ardith uttered a barely intelligible response. "No," she murmured, "I don't." Then she asked, "What happened, where is mama?" In the coming days, Ardith's question became a common refrain.

In all likelihood, this snippet of conversation took place only in the mind of an imaginative journalist. The severe head wound, coupled with blood loss and psychological trauma, left her incapacitated and in a virtual comatose state. For days, Ardith Monroe managed to mumble just two words, *mama* and *water*, which she uttered when she wanted a drink.

Within minutes of first finding Ardith curled into a ball on the bedroom floor, Pinnette raced her to Lee Hospital, where she teetered on the edge of death for several days. Even if she survived the physical wounds, doctors doubted she would ever overcome the emotional trauma of what she experienced inside the Monroe home.

While one team of doctors fought to save Ardith's life, another conducted autopsies on the three victims. The postmortems shed further light on the dark crime that occurred in the Monroe bedroom. Bruises on Neva's inner thighs indicated that her killer or killers may have sexually molested her. Doctors at Lee found similar bruising on Ardith's body. The physicians, however, could not reach a consensus about the bruising. Some believed that the killer or killers raped both Monroe girls; others disagreed with this finding.

On Wednesday, September 21, headlines of the triple homicide appeared on the front pages of newspapers across both Michigan and Indiana. Although the possibility of a postmortem sexual assault remained speculative, newspapermen sensationalized their accounts by packaging possibility as fact. Dowagiac residents shuddered when they read the bit about Neva's postmortem sexual assault. Locals began to worry that somewhere in Dowagiac, perhaps next door, a homicidal necrophiliac remained on the loose.

The senseless and frenzied slaughter of the Monroe family caused all sorts of speculation about the slayers. "Was the Monroe family destroyed by some irresponsible maniac, some crazed and ferocious animal whose mind was gone and only blood lust left, some drug-addict who lived in a world of his own distorted dreams?" a *South Bend News-Times* staff correspondent asked in a headline story about the case. "Or was it the deliberate result of a plotting, cunning intelligence with a motive of hatred behind it? The very atrocity… suggests insanity, or a mind nerved to the act by drugs or drink."

After news of the triple homicide broke, hundreds of curious gawkers descended on the scene of the crime. They peered through the kitchen window, where the decomposing groceries still sat on the table—a scene of domestic life frozen in time—but Cass County sheriff Sherman Wyman ordered that the curtain covering the long bedroom window remain shut, shielding the morbidly curious from the sight of blood-drenched bedsheets.

A contingent of detectives from Chicago and South Bend joined local police officers and Cass County deputies in a desperate search for clues. Because most of the evidence inside the house had been tainted, the crack squad of investigators would need to rely on gossip, rumor, hearsay and innuendo for leads.

Using eyewitness statements made by the people who last saw the Monroes alive, the investigators were able to piece together the family's final hours. Sometime in the late afternoon or early evening of Saturday, September 17, Neva and her father encountered two men in downtown Dowagiac. Waving arms, flushed faces and elevated voices hinted at a conversation that had morphed into a confrontation.

Neighbors last reported seeing William and Mary Monroe that evening. The couple seemed happy enough, perhaps because they were about to leave for vacation, which is where the neighbors believed they had gone when the house appeared deserted on Sunday and Monday.

At about the same time neighbors last spotted William and Mary at home, Neva was at a movie theater in Dowagiac with three girlfriends. After the film, her friends said, they began to walk home when Neva bumped into two men she apparently knew. They pulled her aside, and the trio spent a few minutes in hushed conversation. Then at about 11:00 p.m. she continued on her trek home alone. That was the last time anyone saw her alive.

Detectives hypothesized that the crime occurred sometime Saturday night or early Sunday morning, which meant that Ardith remained in the house for at least two and a half days until Grace McKee stumbled upon the crime scene on Tuesday, September 20.

Any hope of solving the murders rested with Ardith Monroe, who remained in a mental stupor in the days after the slaughter of her family. Awakening from a blunt force trauma–induced coma to find her family bludgeoned to death, followed by two days of huddling in the corner of the bedroom with the remains of her family lying a few feet away, left the twelve-year-old in a state of shock. She vacillated in and out of consciousness at Lee Hospital. During her brief periods of cognizance, she repeatedly called out, "What has happened? Where is mama?" Concerned about the fragility of his patient's mental and physical state, Dr. G.B. Herkimer did not allow detectives to question the one surviving eyewitness to the horrific crime.

With Ardith off-limits, detectives turned their attention to another patient of Lee Hospital, Arthur Criffield, whom they believed may have crossed paths with the Monroe family killers and could possibly identify them. On Sunday— the day after the murders—three unidentified men waylaid the sixteen-year-old farm boy on Cass Road. The assailants pummeled Criffield, stole his watch, shot him in the chest and dumped him on the side of the road.

Arthur Criffield owed his life to his suspenders. A steel buckle had deflected the bullet, which would have torn through his heart and killed him instantly. Doctors removed the bullet from the boy's chest, and within a few days, the teenager began to show signs of improvement and appeared headed toward a full recovery. Unfortunately, he could not identify his three attackers.

The lack of an apparent motive for the slayings vexed detectives. Everyone appeared to like Mary Monroe, and no one had an axe to grind with her husband, either. Then detectives learned that Herbert Smith, an occupant of a neighboring shack, held a longstanding grudge against Monroe stemming from an incident three years earlier when Mary Monroe accused him of killing some chickens. Smith also did not like the Monroe girls and at one time fired a shot in the air to scare them away, although he later told investigators that he fired the warning shot to keep Monroe's chickens away from his garden.

Smith suffered from asthma, his wife told investigators, and often took opiate injections to ease the symptoms. On Saturday, he had a fit and needed an injection to calm him. Mrs. Smith insisted her husband spent most of Saturday night in a deep slumber, but she had noticed two men running away from the Monroe house that evening. She did not think much about it at the time but became suspicious when she saw a car speeding down the road around midnight.

Although the opiate injection would have left him insensate at the time of the murders, Smith nevertheless became a prime suspect. Smith's drug use dovetailed nicely with the widely held belief that a "drug fiend" murdered the Monroe family, which led to a theory that Smith murdered his neighbors either during an attempt to rob them for drug money or in a drug-induced fugue.

Suspiciously, Smith left Dowagiac on Monday, September 19, to receive treatment at a sanitarium in Kalamazoo, where detectives arrested him. They brought him to Dowagiac and relentlessly grilled him. Smith insisted he never went anywhere near the Monroe house on Saturday.

Another promising suspect emerged when detectives began to look into seventeen-year-old Neva's background. Exceptionally good-looking, Neva attracted men like a bright light attracts insects on a hot summer night. Her legion of admirers included a married man twice her age. Thirty-five-year-old William Kinney lived with his wife and eleven-year-old daughter in a home situated between the Monroes' residence and Dowagiac. According to neighborhood yentas, a parade of young girls went into and out of the Kinney house. At some point, it appeared, Neva Monroe joined the parade. They would have made an odd couple: the tall, svelte, teenage beauty and the short, squat, middle-aged married man. Detroit journalists Ralph Goll and Donald F. Schram, who wrote about the case as part of a 1943 series on unsolved homicides, described Kinney as "four feet and eight inches tall" and suffering from a "spinal deformity." According to the *Dowagiac Daily News*, Kinney stood five feet six inches tall and had "stooped shoulders."

The attractive teenager had apparently caught Kinney's eye, and a friendship formed that, according to local gossip, quickly morphed into something more. William Monroe blanched at the thought of his teenager's involvement with the older, married man, which reportedly led to more than one confrontation between the two men. Neva subsequently left school for about a year due to an "illness," which, according to the rumor mill, was a cover story for pregnancy.

Local gossip had William Kinney fathering Neva's child, whom she took to the Michigan Children's Home in St. Joseph shortly after the birth. Investigators pored through the institution's files but found no paper trail for Neva's baby. In the Monroe residence, however, Sheriff Wyman discovered an interesting clue about Neva's possible motherhood: a scrap of paper with a few notes written in Neva's hand. The notes compared a baby to an acorn from an oak tree.

The pernicious rumor of the middle-aged hunchback impregnating his teenaged neighbor remained a thing of small-town gossip. For locals, the illegitimate child provided a logical explanation for William Kinney's hasty departure from Dowagiac around Thanksgiving 1920—according to Goll and Schram, "shortly after the birth of her [Neva's] baby."

Three locals thought he might have been one of the men involved in the confrontation with William and Neva on the night of the murders. The altercation, which supposedly took place in downtown Dowagiac, became loud enough for passersby to hear. The dispute occurred when William told one of the men to stay away from Neva. Enraged, the man responded with an ominous threat: "If you ever bring this matter up again, I'll kill your whole family." Detectives could not verify the story but nonetheless decided to bring in William Kinney and his brother Edward for questioning.

Cass County sheriff Sherman Wyman arrested William Kinney on his farm near Temple, Michigan, and lodged him in the county jail; Edward Kinney voluntarily made the trip to Dowagiac from South Bend to answer questions about his presence in the city the weekend of the Monroe murders. Standing six feet tall and weighing 190 pounds, Edward Kinney said that he had come to Dowagiac to visit an aunt but admitted that he briefly talked with Neva and her father on Saturday night.

William Kinney vehemently denied ever having an intimate relationship with Neva Monroe. Wyman repeatedly grilled him on the widespread belief that he had fathered Neva's child, but Kinney denied every word of it. If Neva left school in the spring of 1920 to give birth to a child, Kinney insisted, it was not his.

What at first appeared a promising line fizzled when both Kinney brothers presented alibis for the night of the triple murder. Edward spent the weekend with a friend, and despite rumors to the contrary, William Kinney was not even in Dowagiac on Saturday. After checking and rechecking every facet of the stories and interviewing dozens of witnesses, police released both men.

Two other persons of interest emerged when Wyman managed to identify the two men seen talking with Neva after she left the picture show in Dowagiac. Twenty-four-year-old Earl Smith and his twenty-two-year-old companion George Means briefly spoke with Neva that night. Means asked Neva if he could walk her home. She declined the offer, and they parted ways. The men managed to convince the sheriff that they had nothing to do with the murders, so Wyman released them. When Smith and Means left custody, Wyman ran out of leads. The case went cold.

After several hours of lingering between life and death, Ardith Monroe began to improve. Doctors who once doubted her survival now expected her to make a full recovery. She regained consciousness and, little by little, began to speak in complete sentences rather than in scrambled bunches of utterances.

She could not recall anything about the attack. She remembered taking a shower at around 9:00 p.m. on Saturday night. The next thing she remembered was waking up and asking her father, "Isn't it time for Sunday school?" but he did not reply. Unbeknownst to Ardith, she had been unconscious for two days. Blind from the head wounds, she could not see why her father had not answered her.

Ardith was able to dispel some of the rumors floating around Dowagiac about the murders. As far as she knew, no one harbored a grudge against her family, and her father did not cache any loot on the property.

About a month later—in November—Ardith created a small sensation when she named a man she said she saw standing over the bed of her mother and father. She admittedly did not know if she saw this man during the crime or during a dream. So scrambled was Ardith's memory of the traumatic event and its aftermath that she had named one of the physicians who tirelessly worked to save her life at the Lee Hospital. Sheriff Wyman did not release "Mr. X's" name, so newspapers referred to him as "a prominent professional man." Newspaper reporters later identified the "prominent professional man" as the Monroe family physician, Dr. Sherman Loupee.

Wyman followed up on Ardith's new "memory," but as he expected, the lead went nowhere. Bits and pieces of memories had apparently become entangled in Ardith's mind. She had confused the memory of Dr. Loupee standing over her hospital bed with her imagined vision of the killer standing over her at the crime scene.

The case appeared on the cusp of closure in late November when a new suspect emerged in the form of Cyrus Ryther, an individual described as "feeble-minded" and dubbed the "Dowagiac moron" by the press. The twenty-year-old had been arrested for what one reporter described as "a particularly revolting type of moral crime," and during interrogation, he shocked his inquisitors by confessing to one of the bloodiest crimes in Cass County history. On Saturday, November 26, 1921, Ryther confessed to the "triple club" slayings.

The crime, Ryther said, resulted from a snatch of conversation he overheard during which Monroe told a neighbor about a cache of $1,500 he had stashed in the shack. Ryther and an individual he identified as "a Polish boy" went to the Monroe house to steal the money. Ryther promptly led Sheriff Wyman to the Monroe cottage, where he provided a graphic narration of the crime.

While the "Polish boy" waited by the road, Ryther said, he peeped in the window. "I saw the older girl taking a bath," Ryther explained, "and tried the front door, opened it and walked into the room. I sat down on a chair beside the door, but when the girl got through and saw me she told me to get out of the house. I went, but wasn't going to be scared by a girl, so I watched until she went to bed. She hadn't locked the door, and so I hadn't any trouble. But before I went in this time, I went around to the back of the house and got a 2x4 sapling out of the wood pile. The lamp was still lighted in the sitting room, and I had lots of light. I went right into the bedroom and put them all out of business in no time."

During the clubbing, he said, Ardith awoke and screamed, "Don't you hurt my mother!" Ryther slapped Ardith across the face before hitting her with the chunk of timber.

Then, he said, he took a lamp and went into the cellar to search for the stash of money. "I looked around the cellar and found a box on the shelf, I put my hand into it, and found a roll of bills. Before leaving the bedroom, I had searched Monroe's pockets and had found a five-dollar bill. I took this with the ones I discovered in the cellar and came upstairs and out of the back door."

He and the unnamed "Polish boy" then buried the cash behind the house. Wyman and his deputies probed the spot where Ryther said they buried Monroe's cache, but they did not find a single bill. When Wyman asked Ryther what he thought happened to the money, the suspect said he thought the "Polish boy" had returned and unearthed it.

At first glance, Ryther's story fit the known facts. He described how he had broken a lamp against a support beam in the cellar of the Monroe home at the precise spot where, two months earlier, investigators had found fragments of broken glass. He also accurately described the position of each victim as found by neighbors.

And his story of slapping Ardith aligned with her fragmented memory of a man (whom she had errantly identified as Dr. Sherman Loupee, the family physician) slapping her across the face. Dr. Loupee's build matched Ryther's, which suggested that Ardith, suffering the effects of significant head trauma, had mistaken the man who clubbed her with a man of similar appearance who later treated her at the hospital.

Yet one aspect of Ryther's story made little sense. If he went to the house to steal Monroe's stash, why would he turn around and bury it on the property instead of taking it with him? Ryther's entire story about the stash seemed far-fetched bordering on fantastic: a king's ransom of $1,500—a huge amount of money at the time—hoarded by a laborer who inhabited a small shack, then stolen, reburied and subsequently unearthed by a nameless accomplice.

Ryther also appeared confused. He confessed to crimes committed by other individuals and admitted to robbing stores that had not been robbed. A *Herald-Press* reporter described the suspect's demeanor during the "confession": "He is continually modifying or amplifying it, and once during the recital of the facts he interrupted himself, and declared that he was telling lies, and that he had obtained all his knowledge of the murder from the newspapers."

Although the "confession" came from a mentally unstable individual, the complete lack of new leads or viable suspects and desperation prompted investigators to take the "Dowagiac moron" at his word. Cornered by a reporter on the jailhouse steps, Sheriff Wyman admitted his suspicions about Ryther's "confession."

"The story sounds very doubtful to me," Wyman admitted.

"Do you believe he committed the murder," the anonymous reporter asked, "or that he merely wants to be notorious?"

"I don't know," Wyman responded.

"Did he impress you, when you were taking him over the scene of the crime with having been there before?"

"I have no doubt he was there before, but whether before or after the crime I cannot say."

"Does he stick to the main facts of his story?"

"He became more confused in telling it all the time."

The unnamed reporter did not wait for an official verdict about Ryther's credibility, instead relying on town gossip. "Citizens who know the prisoner declare that little credence can be placed in his story. They declare that he will plead guilty to anything he is asked about, and that he is utterly without responsibility."

After spending two days behind bars in the Cass County jail, Cyrus Ryther retracted his confession. He witnessed the murders, he said, but the "Polish boy," whom he identified as Wallace Leopowski, had swung the club.

Assistant Attorney General O.L. Smith, at the request of local authorities, traveled from Lansing to Dowagiac to conduct a one-man grand jury into the Monroe murders. After probing Leopowski's alibi, he was convinced the "Polish boy" had nothing to do with the crime.

By January, Smith had concluded the same thing about Cyrus Ryther, whose confession now appeared to be the conjuring of a deranged fantasist. A local judge ordered Ryther confined to the "Lapeer home for feeble-minded." Although cleared of the murder charge, Ryther could not stay out of trouble. In February 1927, he was caught after stealing tools from the barn of a local farmer and damaging two prize mares with a pitchfork. A month later, he pleaded guilty to bootlegging, which brought a sentence of five to ten years in the State Penitentiary at Jackson.

Ryther ended up in the State Hospital for the criminally insane in 1936. When his sentence expired in April 1937, he was recommitted. Whatever he knew, or did not know, about the Monroe murders he took to the grave when he died in 1978.

The case remained in limbo until 1927, when Detective Lyle Morse and Detective Lieutenant Philip Hutson of the Michigan State Police identified a new suspect in the six-year-old-case: John Williams, an inmate of the Indiana State Prison.

In 1921, Williams rented a room in a Dowagiac boardinghouse. His landlady told Morse and Hutson that Williams left the house on Saturday evening and did not return until around four o'clock the following morning. According to the landlady, on Tuesday morning Williams told her about the slaughter of the Monroe family during a brief conversation that, she said, took place just before Grace McKee discovered the crime scene.

Williams said he spent the evening of September 17 playing poker, but his alibi contained holes. Some of his poker-playing associates said they did not remember him in the game. Still, the state police detectives knew that alcohol and time could dull memories. Without something more concrete, they could not make a case against Williams.

Rumors die hard. In the weeks after the "Spiked Club Triple Murders," fortune hunters took apart the Monroe residence board by board and cratered the property searching for William Monroe's lost loot. Like investigators, they came up empty-handed.

2

The Ferndale Head Case

(Ferndale, 1927)

In February 1927, a boy exploring a makeshift storage area above the rafters of a shack in Ferndale made a ghastly discovery that began an investigation into an unidentified fiend known only as the Ferndale "Ghoul." The mystery led to the gallows of a Mississippi jail, where a jerk of the rope ensured the silence of a shadowy character who took the secret of the Ferndale skulls to his grave.

Jeff Hollis had just moved his family into a small shack at 266 Reimanville Avenue in an area known as "Zigaboo Town," a predominantly African American community on the edge of Ferndale. The flimsy structure, owned by a Detroiter named Sally Robinson, consisted of a bare-bones frame covered with tar paper.

Jeff's twelve-year-old son Henry spent his first few days in Ferndale exploring every inch of his new home, except for a dusty attic separated from the main living area by a trapdoor. His father did not want him poking around the rat-infested crawlspace. For a twelve-year-old, the allure of the forbidden room proved too powerful to resist. On Tuesday, February 8, he finally decided to go against his father's commandment by crawling through the trapdoor. At the back of the attic, he found a trunk that contained four circular objects, like small globes, wrapped in old

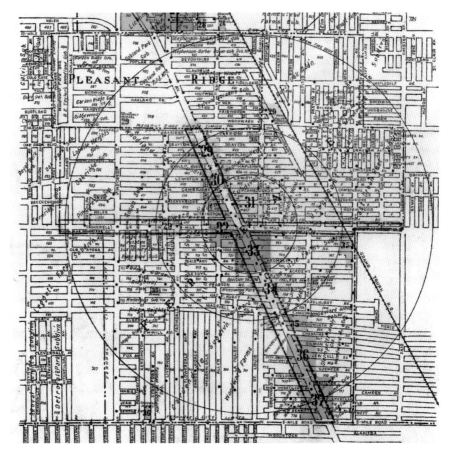

Portion of 1926 Sanborn Fire Insurance Map showing Ferndale. A trunk containing four skulls was found in a shack on Reimanville Road, located in the lower left corner of this map. *Library of Congress Geography and Map Division.*

newspapers. Gently peeling away the newspaper over one of the objects, Henry discovered a human head.

Jeff Hollis reported Henry's find to his landlady the next morning. Sally Robinson promptly informed Ferndale chief of police George Smith, who dispatched officers to bring the trunk to the station.

The official opening of the trunk must have left quite an impression on Smith and the other officers. Four nearly skeletonized human heads, all of which came from women, were neatly wrapped in yellowed newspapers from Cleveland, Detroit and Pittsburgh, and dated from 1921 to 1925. Wrapped around two of the skulls were locks of human hair—one blond and one brunette—each attached to a flap of skin apparently excised with a thin, sharp blade like a boning or a paring knife. The blond scalp contained dried clots of blood.

Were the heads evidence of grave robbery or of murder? An indentation on the lower part of the occipital bone on one of the skulls, caused by a blunt instrument, led Oakland County coroner Albert Crossby to conclude the latter. The bloody braids of hair supported his conclusion that, sometime about two years earlier, four women were murdered and their heads cleaved from their torsos with surgical precision.

The box also held a World War I army tunic, an array of medals, some European coins and a sheaf of papers listing the names, addresses and telephone numbers of women known to move in high-society circles of Pittsburgh and Detroit. One list was named "special group."

Sally Robinson remembered the trunk as the property of her former tenant James H. Coyner, who roomed at 266 Reimanville Avenue until September 1926, when he moved out. "He stored it in the attic and never afterward opened it to my knowledge," Robinson said, adding that she had simply forgotten about it.

Robinson and her husband, Earle, first met Coyner around 1920 as a boarder in their Detroit home. When the Robinsons moved to Royal Oak Township, Coyner moved out. He reappeared in July 1926 and for the next few months lived with the Robinsons at the 266 Reimanville Avenue address while he worked at a local cement factory. One afternoon that summer, Coyner went to Detroit and returned with the trunk, which he tucked into the attic, where it gathered dust until Henry Hollis pried open its lid seven months later. According to Robinson, Coyner never even mentioned the box.

Thirty-five-year-old James H. Coyner was a mystery even to his cohabitants. A hulking giant of a man standing six feet, six inches and with the build of a heavyweight boxer, he was an introvert more comfortable in silence than in conversation. Because Coyner never spoke about himself, Sally Robinson knew virtually nothing about her two-time tenant, his background, his whereabouts or his trunk full of macabre trophies.

Discovering James Coyner became a real feat of detective work for Chief Smith and Oakland County prosecutor Clyde Underwood. Letters found in the trunk suggested that he originally came to Detroit from Boyle, Mississippi, and at some point lived in Pittsburgh, where he apparently collected names and addresses of high-society women, organizing several into a "special group" list for some unknown purpose. One early theory had Coyner stalking these women, but during subsequent police interviews, none of them mentioned harassment of any sort. A corollary had Coyner as a Peeping Tom or "porch-climber" in the era's nomenclature, and the lists of addresses represented a roadmap of his nocturnal activities. While living in Ferndale, Coyner was arrested for "window peeping," which lent some credibility to the theory.

Coyner briefly worked for the Ford Motor Company. In July 1926, he took a job in a cement factory and lived with the Robinsons until he lost his job the following September and left the area. Mrs. Robinson did not know where he went, but a few months later, she received a letter from a friend containing a newspaper clipping that detailed Coyner's arrest in Indiana. That was the last she knew about the mysterious lodger.

From Detroit, Coyner went to Lansing, Illinois, where he worked on a construction crew during the summer of 1926. That fall, he was pinched for robbing a grave in the neighboring community of Hammond, Indiana.

In early October, some kids poking around the concrete foundation of a vacant home site stumbled upon a skeleton filched from the surreptitiously opened grave of Elizabeth See, a twenty-one-year-old woman interred ten years earlier in Oak Hill Cemetery. Police nabbed Coyner when he returned for the body. Asked about his motive, Coyner offered a simple explanation. "I had never seen a dead body and wanted to satisfy my curiosity." He said that he planned to take the body back to Lansing, Illinois.

Sheriff Ben Strong, who was in charge of Coyner, described his prisoner as a dangerous man. "This fellow Coyner, though not surly, is a dangerous man to have charge of. He has the strength of three ordinary men and is forever looking for an opportunity to make a getaway. We've got to keep an eye on him all the time."

The body snatcher became an object of morbid fascination. A *Lake County Times* correspondent described Coyner as a "giant" and characterized his crimes in racially charged language that equated him with a gorilla. "With his naked hands," wrote the unnamed journalist, "[he] lifted the fragile remains…from its final resting place in Oak Hill cemetery and carried it away as would an ape in the jungle." The court sentenced Coyner to three to ten years for the "felonious removal of a corpse."

Smith and Underwood tracked Coyner to the Indiana State Prison in Michigan City, Indiana, where he was serving his sentence for the Hammond, Indiana grave robbery.

Upon receiving a telephone call from the Michigan investigators, Warden E.H. Daly, who characterized Coyner as "mentally deficient," questioned his prisoner about the Ferndale skulls. Coyner admitted to owning the trunk but insisted he knew nothing about either the heads or the bloody braids of hair.

Letters that Coyner penned to his sister in Chicago, however, suggested that he harbored a sinister secret. In one letter, he begged her to go to Detroit and retrieve his trunk, adding, "They may find something else on me and if they do I am through forever." A second letter contained a request for hacksaw blades, so he could saw through the bars of his cell and make a prison break. Again, Coyner added a line that hinted at a mind haunted by the specter of some unmentioned wrongdoing. "You all do not know my trouble," he wrote. "I have not had a chance to tell you. This may not amount to anything here, but there is something else. If that comes against me, I am through forever."

When Smith and Underwood heard about the letters, they made a beeline to Michigan City to grill Coyner about the skulls and his lists of socialites. One central question hung over the investigation: was the owner of the trunk a grave robber or a murderer? Circumstantial evidence paired Coyner with the trunk, and Coyner's conviction for grave robbery raised the possibility that he may have unearthed other graves in other locations not yet established. On the other hand, the bloody lock of hair suggested a more sinister scenario.

By the time Smith and Underwood motored out of the Motor City, Detroit newspapers had already nicknamed James Coyner "the ghoul." Reporters did not hesitate to print grist from the prison rumor mill. "From his prison in Indiana," wrote a *Detroit Free Press* reporter, "he is reported to having admitted a craving for possessing white women's skulls."

Warden Daly believed that his prisoner had confined his illegal activities to bodysnatching only. "It is highly possible, though," the warden said, "that Coyner took those skulls with him when he went to Ferndale last summer. In that case he undoubtedly rifled other graves in this locality." The warden added, "He may tell us about it yet. Then we'll find out where he hid the bodies."

Discovery of the Ferndale skulls triggered parallel investigations in Chicago, South Bend and Toledo. While Smith and Underwood motored east, Cook County officials probed for more hidden bodies, South Bend detectives attempted to link Coyner to an unsolved case of a headless trunk found floating in the St. Joseph River and Toledo police pondered the possibility that Coyner was a fiend known as the "clubber."

Once considered an isolated incident, Coyner's grave robbery in Hammond now appeared to be one event in a possible sequence of either postmortem thefts or murders or both. Because Coyner said he wanted to bring Elizabeth See's body back to his shack in Bernice, near Lansing, Illinois, a theory emerged that had Coyner either murdering four Chicagoland women or robbing four Chicagoland graves. After beheading the corpses, he stashed the remains in and around the shack. Then, he took the heads to Ferndale.

At the direction of Cook County coroner Oscar Wolfe, a squad of detectives descended on the property. Like a team of archaeologists, they sifted through the soil and pried up floorboards. After an exhaustive search, however, they failed to find a single bone.

In South Bend, detectives now viewed Coyner as a prime suspect in the case involving a headless corpse that bobbed to the surface of the St. Joseph River on Thursday, February 10—two days after the discovery of the Ferndale skulls.

The female torso belonged to an unidentified victim whose murderer, authorities believed, sawed off her head before tossing her remains into the river. According to Coroner Carl Reifels, the victim did not die of drowning. She likely went into the water sometime during the late fall or early winter and remained under the surface, because either the icy water slowed the decomposition process that would have caused the body to bloat and float or the body became wedged in an underwater obstacle such as a submerged log.

A person traveling from Ferndale, Michigan, to Lansing, Illinois, would most likely have crossed the St. Joseph River at some point along the way, a fact not lost on detectives who wanted to pin the murder on James Coyner. They envisioned a scenario in which the "ghoul" waylaid the woman, hacked off her head as a trophy and tossed the body into the St. Joseph River, where it popped up four months later. Coyner's arrest in Hammond, Indiana, took place on October 3, and he remained in custody until his trial and sentencing in late November, so he would have had to commit the crime four months earlier. Detroit pathologist Dr. J.L. Hathaway planned to examine the South Bend torso to see if one of the Ferndale skulls matched.

Toledo investigators eyed Coyner as a fiend known as the "clubber," a reportedly huge man who attacked several women in 1926. Because Coyner had been in the area during one of the clubbings, he became the prime suspect in the Ohio series of crimes.

When Smith and Underwood interviewed James Coyner, the cagey prisoner dashed any hopes of a quick resolution when he admitted to owning a trunk similar to the one found in Ferndale but insisted he knew nothing about the ghoulish contents.

"I could tell you lots of things you'd like to know," Coyner said. "But I'll die first."

"If I wanted to," Coyner bragged, "I could tell you about a lot of murders and murderers. There are plenty of them walking around the streets of Detroit that you want, but I won't talk."

That he wanted to make a deal for reduced prison time became evident in his next statement, a thinly veiled attempt to act as if he did not want a release, a ploy he may have intended as both a feeler and a piece of reverse psychology.

"I'm a defiant fellow. You can't get a thing out of me. It will be time for me to talk when I get out of prison ten years from now," Coyner continued, "but I don't care about getting out. There is no justice in the world. I'd rather be in Africa, in the jungles, where there's no fear of the law."

If Coyner was selling, Smith and Underwood weren't buying. Instead, the sheriff and prosecutor left the Indiana State Penitentiary more convinced than ever that the Ferndale ghoul held guilty information about numerous crimes, so they decided to redouble their efforts.

"Coyner was very defiant," Chief Smith said of the interviewee after their first meeting. "When we questioned him about the contents of the trunk he would shoot us a leering grin, and say: 'It's your business to find that out.'" The prisoner's defiance prompted Smith and Underwood to rethink their tactics. Perhaps when confronted with the skulls, they reasoned, Coyner would crack. The Detroit lawmen sent for the four decollated heads, which came across the state in the back seat of Oakland County deputy sheriff Frank Greenan's car.

Smith and Underwood had misjudged the prisoner, who viewed the skulls with a grin. When they dangled the blood-streaked scalp in front of him, however, Coyner flinched. Visibly agitated, he recoiled at the sight of the hair, sprang to his feet and screeched, "Take it away! Take it away!"

To the dismay of the Michigan investigators, the ghastly relics failed to elicit a confession. Surly as ever, Coyner refused to say another word and demanded to be taken back to his cell. Smith believed they were close to unraveling the "ghoul mystery."

"I am convinced, after talking to Coyner," he told reporters, "that he can fully explain all about those four skulls, and I am also satisfied that he will confess to murder before we are through."

"When we showed him the blood-stained hair," Smith continued, "he leaped to his feet and cried, 'Take it away, take it away, I don't want to see it.' He was reluctant to talk, but he has admitted he knows a lot and we intend to get it out of him."

Smith, Underwood and Greenan returned to the Motor City but planned to make another cross-state trip to Michigan City for a third interview. Meanwhile, Warden Daly lodged Coyner in a solitary confinement cell.

If Coyner stole the skulls from graves, it was highly unlikely he took them from a Detroit cemetery. Gebhard Schoof, the Detroit Police Department's resident expert on "ghoul" crimes, knew of no disturbed graves in Detroit for the past decade. Schoof had worked three grave robbery cases, the most recent occurring several years earlier, and none of the bodies was mutilated.

Schoof proposed a far-out theory to explain the Ferndale skulls:

> *There seems to be no connection between any ghoul case I ever worked on and the Ferndale case. I strongly believe the Oakland county job is the work of "religious head-hunters." In Africa large bands of "head-hunters" exist, and there is no reason why some of them could not migrate to this country and attempt to practice here. These people have been known to stalk their prey for years, awaiting the opportunity to pounce upon and murder them. My belief is strengthened by the fact that Coyner from his prison cell said he would "rather be in darkest Africa, than loose in the United States."*

The description of James Coyner, which circulated on the front pages of all the Detroit dailies, sounded remarkably familiar to retired Detroit detective lieutenant Warren C. Richardson, who busted William Cantrell, the self-proclaimed "king of ghouls," for armed robbery in 1915. Cantrell, who called himself a preacher, ran a shelter out of his small home on Catherine Street. In the winter, people in need of a warm place to sleep could come into Cantrell's shelter and listen to his preaching. When they nodded off to sleep, Cantrell and his partner in crime Eldridge Gowdy filched jewelry and whatever else of value they found on these transients. Richardson busted Cantrell, who received two years in Jackson for the scheme.

"Cantrell told me he was conducting the mission to atone for his sins in Indiana," Richardson recalled. "He said he robbed lots of graves there. He boasted of it." Apparently, his nocturnal excavations were a source of pride. When sentenced, Cantrell stood up in court, threw his arms into the air and proclaimed, "I am the king of the ghouls."

Coyner's cryptic remark about knowing "a lot of murders and murderers...walking around the streets of Detroit" made Richardson wonder if the four Ferndale skulls originated with the "king of ghouls."

Ultimately, however, the case fell flat when James Coyner refused to talk. Like a fencer, he parried all of the thrusts of Smith and Underwood. Apart from the possible charge of looting graves, the Oakland County men had nothing on him. They knew it, he knew it and they knew that he knew it.

Coyner returned to the general prison population, and the case of the Ferndale skulls grew colder with each passing day. The "ghoul mystery" faded from the front pages and became nothing more than a memory of an intriguing case until 1934, when James Coyner once again made the front pages...in Mississippi.

James Coyner had served seven years and seven months in the Indiana State Penitentiary at Michigan City when he left on parole in the spring of 1934 and drifted east to Cleveland, Ohio.

On September 5, a boy exploring the shore of Lake Erie near Euclid Beach stumbled upon the headless, armless trunk of an unidentified female. Her killer had applied a chemical agent to her skin, which made it appear red in color. After examining the remains, Cuyahoga County coroner Dr. Arthur J. Pearse concluded that the killer had cured his victim's flesh. Investigators never found the head and never managed to identify the woman nicknamed the "Lady of the Lake."

That fall, several affluent female denizens of Indianapolis received obscene letters—many of them containing threats of bodily harm—postmarked Cleveland, Mississippi. Complaints about the blue mail led to a federal investigation, and a postal inspector began nosing around the small Mississippi town.

The postmarks indicated that the sender used the Cleveland, Mississippi post office. Postal inspector T.D. Rock reasoned that the author of the lewd letters might have obtained the names of Indianapolis socialites from a newspaper. The hunch paid off when a man appeared at the post office to pick up his mail, which included an Indianapolis newspaper.

Rock and Bolivar County sheriff deputy Charles Maddox nabbed the suspect in January 1935 as he stepped into the post office. During a routine search, sheriff's deputies found Aurelius Turner's watch in one of the suspect's pockets and an envelope containing a chunk of Louella Turner's salted flesh in another. These trophies tied the blue letter writer to a horrific crime that had rocked the small town of Cleveland, Mississippi, a month earlier. On December 8, 1934, an unknown assailant crept in the Turner residence and brained Aurelius Turner and his expectant wife, Louella, with an axe before mutilating her remains.

The man gave his name as "James H. Coyner," but when Maddox conducted a probe into the suspect's background, he discovered that Coyner was born Alonzo Robinson. The deputy sheriff also learned that Robinson's penchant for writing dirty letters apparently began years earlier. A native of the Cleveland, Mississippi area, Robinson fled the state following an incident during which a local farmer, upon discovering a lewd letter that Robinson wrote to his wife, shot him.

As he had done in Michigan City, Coyner at first denied any wrongdoing with a nonchalance bordering on haughtiness, but a search of his house uncovered damning evidence, including fifty-two obscene letters and salted portions of Mrs. Turner's skin, pocked with teeth marks (he later admitted to chewing on the strips of skin but would not explain why). Fearing a lynch mob, authorities moved Coyner to the Hinds County Jail in Jackson.

Faced with overwhelming physical evidence of his guilt, Coyner decided to talk and summoned the sheriff to his cell. He attacked the Turners, he admitted, because he experienced a sudden compulsion to kill, and he butchered Louella Turner because he wanted to know how her skin felt. Then he gave a detailed, blow-by-blow account of the Turner murders to the sheriff and prosecuting attorney and later repeated the confession for a third time in front of an audience of stunned reporters.

About twenty officers and newspaper reporters crammed into the Hinds County Jail to listen to James Coyner describe the "fiendish brutality" that took place inside the Turner residence. The Jackson, Mississippi *Daily Clarion-Ledger* characterized the case "as amazing a story of crime and fiendish brutality as was ever recorded" and described the perpetrator as a "gingerbread Deltan of strong body and perverted mind."

He had, he admitted, attacked Aurelius Turner as he read a newspaper in the living room and his wife, Louella, as she dozed in bed alongside her two sons (ten-year-old daughter Merline Turner spent the night at a friend's house). He struck four-year-old Aurelius Jr. in the head with an axe but left two-year-old Jimmy unharmed.

Coyner described the murders with the detached tone of someone describing a trip to the corner market. "I sneaked up behind Mr. Turner with the hatchet and hit him over the head as he turned and lunged for his gun," Coyner said without a hint of emotion in his voice. "The woman screamed and I stepped over and hit her three or four times over the head. Then I grabbed the gun and shot Mr. Turner through the head."

After slicing off pieces of flesh from Mrs. Turner's arms, back and buttocks and wrapping them in newspaper, Coyner disemboweled her, ripping the unborn baby from its mother's womb and laying it on the bed beside her. He went to bed that night, he said, without washing his hands.

The Mississippi murders revived interest in the Ferndale "ghoul mystery," and James Coyner once again made headlines in the Motor City. Detective John I. Navarre of the Detroit Homicide Squad planned to send a facsimile set of fingerprints taken from the Evangelist crime scene to determine if Coyner had anything to do with the 1929 slaughter of the Detroit occultist and his entire family (see chapter 4, "The St. Aubin Avenue House of Horrors").

According to some newspaper reports, during the admissions spree in Mississippi, Coyner alluded to unearthing the four skulls from graves around

Ferndale, but since he never told police where he exhumed them or what happened to the rest of their bodies, his confession fell short of solving the "ghoul mystery." After the Mississippi story broke, some investigators concluded that Coyner ate the bodies.

During an interview with District Attorney Greek L. Rice in Mississippi, Coyner said he obtained the skulls by robbing graves in Michigan and offered a motive of sorts. "I did it to get the bones," he said. "The heads were the only things in the graves." He failed to provide any specifics, however, and never accounted for the blood-stained locks of hair found with the skulls.

The confession Coyner gave in Mississippi, however, did clear up one aspect of the Ferndale mystery. He admitted to penning obscene letters sent to the wives and daughters of affluent Indianapolis residents, which indicated how he used the "special group" of names and addresses found in his trunk in Ferndale. Since Coyner never explained his motive for sending such letters, this facet of his behavior remains shrouded in mystery.

The emotionally charged trial took place on February 14, 1935. To keep a lynch mob from cheating the hangman, a contingent of five hundred National Guardsmen barricaded the courtroom doors with sandbags and stood watch over the proceedings.

It took a jury just five minutes to deliberate and return a verdict of guilty. After listening to the judge pronounce a sentence of death by hanging, Coyner responded with a blood-curdling laugh that shocked spectators.

Up until the moment of Coyner's execution, officers attempted to ferret out information about his other possible crimes, including the Ferndale heads, but he kept his promise "to carry [his] secrets to the grave."

The "ghoul" took the long walk to the gallows situated on the top floor of the Bolivar County Jail on Tuesday, March 5, 1935, at 3:50 a.m. *Clarion-Ledger* staff writer James B. Gibson described the climactic moment in his morning-after front-page story: "A quick jerk of the sheriff's hand and the trap on which the prisoner stood swung backward and free. The body of Robinson dropped through the aperture, fully six feet before the rope became taut."

True to his word, Coyner died without revealing where, when and how he had obtained the Ferndale skulls.

Coyner's connection with the "Lady of the Lake" also remains a tantalizing, unsolved mystery. Seven months after Coyner dropped from the gallows—on September 23, 1935—the headless bodies of two men were found in Cleveland. Some researchers consider these two as the first in a sequence known as the "Cleveland Torso Murders," which ended with the discovery of the twelfth victim in 1938. Other students of the case believe that the first true victim was the "Lady of the Lake."

Unless Coyner returned from the grave, he could not have perpetrated the "Cleveland Torso Murders," but he could have been responsible for the "Lady of the Lake."

While Coyner confessed to murder in Mississippi, he never copped to anything other than grave robbery in Michigan and Indiana. The slaying of the Turner couple, however, proved that he could—and did—murder. Yet even at the eleventh hour, when the clock ticked off the last minutes of his life and he no longer needed to fear further charges in other jurisdictions, the man who so freely detailed the murder and mutilation of the Turners remained mute about other crimes.

The statement Coyner made from his cell in Michigan City, Indiana, which simultaneously titillated, baffled and frustrated Michigan investigators, leads to another intriguing possibility. "I could tell you about a lot of murders and murderers," Coyner bragged. "There are plenty of them walking around the streets of Detroit that you want, but I won't talk."

Did Coyner know the identity of the person responsible for the Toledo Club crimes, the South Bend torso victim, the Lady of the Lake and later the Cleveland Torso Murders? Did this unidentified serial killer pay for Coyner's silence with body parts from his victims? Or did Coyner work in tandem with this unknown killer by dumping the bodies in waterways after first removing the heads, which he collected?

The Ferndale Ghoul left more questions than answers.

3

The Doctor, His Wife and the Other Woman

(Detroit, 1927)

I n May 1927, the front pages belonged to Lucky Lindy and his *Spirit of St. Louis*, but in Detroit, columns devoted to the famous aviator's transatlantic flight appeared side-by-side with columns detailing the trial of a local doctor embroiled in one of the most baffling murder mysteries in Motor City history. Some considered it the perfect crime.

Even the best detectives in the city—hardened dicks who traded lead with gangsters, bootleggers and rumrunners—could not crack the case of the doctor, his wife and the "other woman." It was a tantalizing story of duality, forbidden love and betrayal set against the backdrop of Prohibition-era Detroit.

The first blow dropped Grace Loomis to her knees and opened a gash on her scalp over her left temple. As she knelt on the rug like a woman in prayer, her killer raised his club with a violent recoil that threw a castoff stain against the wallpaper and window drapes. He brought the club down on her head a second time, the wood striking skull with the sound of a dull thud. She flopped to the floorboards between two wicker chairs in the sunroom, her body trembling with convulsions. Two more blows, and she lay still, a halo of blood forming around her battered cranium. Thirty-four-year-old Grace Burns Loomis, mother of two and wife of a prominent Detroit physician, was dead.

The stealth attack took Grace Loomis completely by surprise. Sounds of the attack—a hoarse whispered cry, a muffled screech, the shuffling of feet—did not reach a level to wake eight-year-old Frank Jr. and six-year-old Jeannette, who were asleep upstairs.

At approximately 9:30 p.m., Dr. Frank Loomis waltzed through the front door of his Dutch Revival home at 13901 Marlowe Avenue. About forty-five minutes earlier, he had gone for his customary stroll despite the light but steady rain that began falling earlier that evening. Brushing the drizzle from his coat, he thought about calling out to Grace, but the children would be fast asleep and he did not want to wake them. He peeled off his overshoes and went into the sunroom, where he found Grace, her head pulped by some blunt weapon, lying in a pool of blood on the floorboards near the davenport.

He darted across the room, fell to his knees next to the still figure of his wife and felt for a pulse. When he realized that the only sound he heard was the throbbing of his own heart, he raced to the phone. It appeared to be out of order, so he went onto the back porch and yelled to a neighbor, Mildred Twork.

Mrs. Twork was getting ready to go to bed when she heard Loomis calling her name. She went to the bedroom window and asked what Loomis wanted. "My wife has been murdered," he yelled. "Please call the police and come right over."

Loomis then sprinted to the Schoolcraft police station, arriving at about 9:50 p.m., where he gave a second recitation of events. "Please come on quick," he squelched. "There's been a murder. Someone has murdered my wife." With Sergeant Milford Harrison and Patrolman Elijah Wasson in tow, Loomis returned to his home.

As soon as the officers entered the house, they noticed a drastic temperature change. Harrison described it as a blast of heat in the face. Despite unseasonably warm temperatures for February in Michigan, someone had stoked the cellar furnace and closed all of the windows.

Harrison examined the furnace. "The draft was open," he later recalled. "I opened the front door and found it fueled to the door's edge and it was burning freely." Someone had apparently just stoked the furnace because much of the coal remained uncharred.

Mildred Twork entered the front door a few minutes later. The bloody scene in the sunroom nearly unhinged Twork, who later recalled, "I had to sit down until I came to." When she regained her senses, she thought about the Loomis children. "Are the children alright?" she asked.

"You don't think…" Loomis responded. This was the first time that anyone heard him express concern for the safety of his two children that night. Loomis and Patrolman Elijah Wasson ran up the stairs to find Frank Jr. and Jeanette still fast asleep.

News of the crime traveled quickly, and within an hour, Detective Lieutenant Frank McNally arrived at 13901 Marlowe Avenue with a squad of six homicide detectives. Wiping sweat beads from their brows, the detectives began searching for evidence. The scene in the sunroom suggested a violent struggle. An overturned chair lay on its back, and blood spatter dotted the window coverings and wallpaper near the body of Grace Loomis. Shards of glass from a fractured window had fallen onto the front lawn, indicating that it had been broken from the inside, possibly when one of the two figures had smashed into it during the struggle. Oddly, a telephone sat on the floor with its receiver in place.

Certain aspects of the scene led McNally to conclude that the killer had attempted to cover his tracks by obliterating evidence. Blood spots on the kitchen sink hinted that the killer washed his hands, possibly to avoid the mistake of leaving bloody fingerprints at the scene of the crime. (Later, Deputy Coroner George Berg admitted that he used the sink to wash blood from his hands after examining Grace Loomis's body.)

Once the red-hot coals in the furnace cooled, the detectives sifted through the ashes and found two charred pearl buttons, suggesting that the killer stoked the fire and reduced incriminating evidence, such as a blood-soaked shirt, into dust. Detectives also found a syringe filled with morphine, although at the time it did not raise any eyebrows since Loomis practiced medicine for a living.

McNally quickly eliminated two obvious motives. Grace Loomis was fully clothed, and the postmortem revealed no indications of a sexual assault. Robbery also seemed out of the question. Except for a one-hundred-dollar bill Loomis said he gave to his wife, nothing was missing. The three rings that Grace Loomis wore were still on her fingers.

Loomis, however, theorized that the one-hundred-dollar note might have doomed his wife. When he handed the money to Grace, he suggested, perhaps someone had watched from the undrawn blinds of the sunroom. When he left for his evening walk, the perpetrator sneaked into the house and attacked his wife.

The crafty homicide detective allowed Dr. Loomis to search the house for clues alongside his men, although he made sure that he was never out of sight. The search for clues became an impromptu interrogation as Loomis's shadows pelted him with questions about his movements that night. At some point, Loomis must have recognized their attempts to catch him in a lie. "Gentlemen," he protested, "I am telling you everything. I wish I could tell you more. I am more eager than you to clear up the slaying."

Photographs of Loomis became front-page fixtures in February 1927. *Author's collection.*

During the first twenty-four hours of the investigation, McNally's team of investigators spoke to several eyewitnesses who provided vital information about the sequence of events that occurred inside the Loomis residence that night. Florence Nellis, who lived at 13391 Marlowe, heard the crashing of glass at approximately 9:05 p.m. She could fix the time because it occurred just after she heard the clock strike nine. "I was lying in bed when I heard our clock strike nine and I counted the strokes," Nellis later recalled. "It must have been five minutes later that I heard the glass break." She called to her brother, fourteen-year-old Harold Simms.

Simms also heard the sounds of breaking glass. About thirty minutes earlier, at approximately 8:30 p.m., he noticed Grace Loomis standing by the sunroom window, which made him the last person to see her alive.

About a half an hour later, Charles Blockson and Ethel Bell happened to walk by the Loomis house and heard muffled screams followed by moaning and the smashing of glass coming from behind the closed blinds of the sunroom. Bell said she heard the screams at about five minutes to nine and described the window shades as about two-thirds drawn.

Bell, who said she stood about fifteen feet away from the house, described the sounds emanating from behind the closed blinds of the sunroom as sharp "screams" that turned into soft "moans." "I felt inside of me that someone was being murdered," Bell related.

She wanted to go to the police, but her walking companion that night, Charles Blockson, believed that either the sounds came from one of Dr. Loomis's patients—a convincing argument since neither he nor Bell heard a man's voice—or they emanated from a family squabble, so they decided not to intervene. They waited outside of the house for a few minutes before continuing on their stroll. "But even after the glass had crashed and the moans ceased," Bell later recalled, "we remained outside the house for at least three minutes, but nobody ran out while we were there. Whoever killed Mrs. Loomis stayed right inside there with the body at least that length of time after the murder."

A telephone operator named Doris McClure said she received two calls that night from Garfield 0800, the Loomis residence. The first call came in sometime between 7:00 p.m. and 8:42 p.m. When McClure asked for a number, a woman's voice on the other end of the line responded, "Never mind, the telephone fell over." At 9:05 p.m., a second call came in from Garfield 0800. When McClure asked for a number this time, no one responded. A few seconds later, she heard a scream and the connection went dead. These witnesses indicated that the murder of Grace Loomis occurred sometime between 8:30 p.m. and 9:00 p.m.

Dr. Loomis's strong-arm theft theory did not explain the closed blinds of the sunroom windows. If the killer seized an opportunity to make a fast hundred bucks, he would not have shut the blinds before the blitz attack on Grace Loomis. He also would not have tried to make a call from the crime scene.

During the ensuing forty-eight hours, Wayne County medical examiner Dr. William D. Ryan performed two postmortems. Under the blood-matted hair on the victim's head were four L-shaped wounds, each with a ragged edge caused by a blunt object. Grace Loomis died of a cerebral hemorrhage, but not before putting up a fight. Several minor wounds—a contusion over her left eye, scratches across her jaw and cuts to both her right arm and left hand—suggested that she had tried to defend herself.

Grace Burns grew up on a farm near Sussex, New Jersey. As a nineteen-year-old nursing student at New York's Metropolitan Hospital, she met dashing twenty-eight-year-old medical intern Frank Loomis. Despite the ten-year age gap, they were both small-town kids in the Big Apple with more than a little in common. A native of Brooklyn, Michigan, Loomis, like the attractive teenage nurse, grew up in a rural, agrarian community. Their whirlwind romance led to the altar in the fall of 1914. A few years later, the young couple moved to Loomis's hometown, where he practiced medicine until they relocated to Detroit in 1924.

By 1927, Dr. Frank Loomis had established a reputation as a skilled anesthetist. The Loomis couple appeared to be living a fairytale romance. Neighbors never heard them quarrel, and Grace adored her husband. "They seemed like the perfect couple," a neighbor recalled. When McNally asked Loomis if his wife might have something on the side, the doctor recoiled and described his wife as the "perfect wife and mother."

Frank McNally knew the adage. In cases of uxoricide, look to the husband first. The annals of Motor City crime contained numerous examples of felonious husbands bumping off their wives to collect on life insurance policies or to make room for new Mrs. While Dr. Loomis had no apparent motive for slaying his wife, the hard evidence pointed in his direction.

Nothing at the scene suggested a break-in. Grace Loomis habitually locked all the doors each night, and when McNally's team first entered the house, they found all of the windows closed and latched. It would have been possible for an intruder to reach in through the milk chute and unlock the exterior door, except the milk chute was closed both on the outside and inside of house. None of the doors were jimmied, and the sunroom window was broken from the inside.

Dr. Loomis's overcoat was streaked with blood, which Loomis easily explained as the result of holding his wife's lifeless body in his arms and frantically probing for a pulse. Curiously, his shirt did not contain a single droplet of blood. The clean shirt, coupled with the charred buttons found among the glowing embers of the furnace, led some detectives to ponder a scenario in which Dr. Loomis returned home from his walk, removed his coat and overshoes and met Grace in the sunroom. He lowered the blinds, and when she turned her back to him, he slugged her in the temple with a club fashioned from a thick piece of wood such as a two-by-four.

He washed his hands in the kitchen sink, burned the blood-drenched shirt and the wooden club in the furnace, put on a new shirt, donned his overcoat and then "found" his wife. This scenario would explain the closing of the blinds that occurred sometime between the Sims and the Blockson/ Bell sightings.

Except Loomis had an alibi. At the time his wife's killer tiptoed behind her, the doctor strutted around the block on his evening stroll. This less-than-perfect alibi, however, put Loomis in the vicinity at the time of the murder.

Throughout the night and early morning of February 23, McNally, Frahm, Detective Lieutenant John Navarre and Assistant Prosecutor Paul O. Buckley attempted to poke holes in Dr. Loomis's alibi. For nearly twenty hours, they quizzed Loomis about his rendition of the previous night's events. The story remained unchanged, its teller undaunted. "I am as innocent as a man can be," he said several times during the grilling.

In a story he repeated an estimated ten times during the interrogation, Loomis said that he came home from his Grand River Avenue office at about 9:00 p.m. He gave Grace a one-hundred-dollar bill to purchase a new coat and left for his evening walk, which he cut short because of the rain. He returned home at about 9:30 p.m. to find his wife battered to death.

When McNally asked Loomis if he had something on the side, the doctor vehemently denied the existence of "the other woman," although he did acknowledge driving a former patient named Gertrude Newell downtown. Police interviewed Newell, but convinced the association was as Loomis presented it, they released her.

Loomis's sangfroid shocked Buckley. "I have never seen a cooler man under such cross-examination than he has been," the assistant prosecutor remarked. Buckley dismissed Loomis's alibi as too neat. "The imperfection of the doctor's story," he said, "is the perfection."

Frahm expressed his frustration with the case. "We have absolutely nothing to indicate that he did the killing and neither have we any information that would indicate that anyone else did it. We are at a total loss to find a motive for the killing."

Despite the apparent lack of motive, by mid-morning of Thursday, February 24, Dr. Frank Loomis faced a possible first-degree murder charge. Detective Paul Wencel escorted the exhausted suspect to a cell.

Loomis's incarceration triggered a fierce courtroom scrap between Buckley and Loomis's lawyer Louis Colombo, who argued that since the police had nothing on his client, they had no right to detain him. Circuit Court judge Joseph A. Moynihan gave the police a twenty-four-hour window in which to present compelling, substantial evidence of Loomis's guilt. If they failed to find anything substantial, they would have to release their one and only suspect. The courtroom drama played to a full house of mostly women who waited in line for over two hours to catch a glimpse of the now-infamous doctor. They craned their necks as Loomis entered the room.

The *Detroit Times* correspondent described the embattled widower. "Freshly shaven and well groomed with clean white linen, Dr. Loomis wore

Dr. Frank Loomis in 1927. Reporters noted his icy, emotionless demeanor during the murder trial. *Author's collection.*

a light tan coat over a blue serge suit and sat expressionless through the arguments, his eyes staring straight ahead always."

Judge Moynihan's imposed deadline of Saturday came and went with no new evidence in the case, but he decided to delay the habeas corpus hearing until Monday, which gave investigators a few more days to gather evidence. A friend of Loomis supplied the $10,000 bond set by Moynihan, and Loomis left custody Saturday afternoon.

Throughout the weekend, a team of homicide investigators sifted every clue recovered from the Loomis residence. They reinterviewed key witnesses. They re-canvassed the neighborhood. Despite their best efforts, they could not locate the murder weapon or other smoking gun type of physical evidence tying Dr. Loomis to the crime scene or a viable motive for the murder of his wife.

On Monday morning, February 28, Judge Moynihan returned the $10,000 bail money, and Loomis walked out of the courtroom a free man. He promptly took his wife's body to her hometown of Newton, New Jersey, for burial. Over the next five weeks, Navarre, Wencel, Frahm and Sergeant James Bogan rubbed elbows with *Detroit Times* reporters and private detectives from the Burns Detective Agency in a relentless search for new evidence. They dug deep into Loomis's life, retraced his steps in the weeks leading up to his wife's murder and interviewed anyone and everyone who knew the doctor. Their quest for clues led to the city's seedy underworld of speakeasies.

When Loomis returned from New Jersey, a squad of detectives shadowed his movements. They tailed him to a small house. A figure—the very image of a voluptuous starlet—answered the door. They had found "G," Dr. Frank Loomis's "other woman."

Enter G. About two weeks into the investigation, detectives discovered a lady friend of Dr. Loomis known as "G," who represented the missing piece in the case against Loomis: a compelling motive for the murder of his wife. She was the same woman Loomis admitted to giving lifts downtown. Considered a casual acquaintance and released after a brief round of questioning, G was more than a former patient, detectives now realized.

Gertrude Newell, called "Nurse" by her friends and "G" by Loomis, was an attractive twenty-nine-year-old divorcée who was the night to Grace Loomis's day. The wild, untamed flapper could not be less like her domesticated counterpart. Wearing her typical housedress, Grace Loomis cooked, cleaned and waited at the front door for her children to come home from school. While Grace slumbered, Gertrude Newell put on her party skirt and high heels and did the Charleston in the city's underground nightclubs.

Photographs of the two women revealed stark contrasts. Conservative, Plain Jane Grace Loomis wore very little makeup. Gertrude Newell, who wore her brick-red hair in a fashionable bob, covered her bee-stung lips with bright-red lipstick. In short, Grace Loomis wore a corset; Grace Newell wore a brassiere. Perhaps the magnetism of this physical beauty mixed with a touch of the exotic and the forbidden proved irresistible to Dr. Loomis.

Newell's marriage to a real estate agent named Ritter ended in 1922 because, Ritter said, his wife "took no interest in their home." By this time, "Nurse" had found a more interesting alternative to domesticity and may have already found her way into Detroit's high life on the arm of a prominent surgeon. Newell's daughter with Ritter, nine-year-old Purnesse, went with her father.

Subsequent investigation into G hinted that she led the life of a high-priced courtesan. Two prominent surgeons, who agreed to speak with authorities only after promises of anonymity, related how they had become entranced by the red-headed siren. Detectives also learned a great deal about "G" from an affluent community and business scion of Highland Park, whose mistress was a close "associate" of Gertrude Newell.

While Loomis tried in vain to keep his relationship with "Nurse" under the covers, the couple went to public gatherings together. It was only a matter of time before investigators learned about Dr. Loomis's other woman.

Investigators uncovered witnesses who told of some strange behavior from Loomis's gal pal in the days after Grace Loomis's murder. Newell and a friend named Bessie Fraser were drinking with two male companions at a blind pig when Newell spotted a newspaper with a front-page story about Loomis's first arrest. She began to sob and buried her head in her hands.

The proprietress noticed the paper on the table and wryly commented, "Dr. Loomis could throw light on that murder." One of the men tailed her to the kitchen. "You shouldn't say that," he chided. "Nurse there is Dr. Loomis's sweetie."

Newell apparently could feel the heat around the corner. According to a neighbor, when she read the *Detroit Times* headline "Woman Sought in Loomis Case," she packed a bag and bolted, leaving town for a few days. Even more suspicious was the telephone operator's report that the voice on the phone call placed from the Loomis residence at about the time of the murder came from a woman.

Detectives traced Loomis's night "Nurse" to Fraser's house and brought her in for questioning. At first, she denied even knowing the doctor but then admitted seeing him once or twice. Eventually, she confessed going to at least a dozen "automobile and drinking parties" with Loomis in the weeks leading up to Grace Loomis's murder.

Their friendship had begun innocently enough. Dr. Loomis first met G the previous November when he treated her for a cold. The more time the doctor spent with G, however, the more his finances suffered. Bank records indicated that over the next few months, the doctor's monthly income sagged from $1,000 to $200. The difference, detectives believed, funded the doctor's alcohol- and possibly drug-fueled nightlife with his mistress. The syringe of morphine found in the Loomis residence may have represented a token of the doctor's newly established Xanadu.

Loomis tried in vain to convince his inquisitors that his relationship with Newell was platonic, but his denials convinced no one. Several times after the murder, detectives tailed him to Fraser's house, where he attempted to see G. Supposedly, when investigators discovered Loomis's interest in Newell, they bugged her residence. What they heard from the listening device never went public, but it probably contained sounds suggesting something more than a casual friendship.

In Detroit's underground watering holes, where whiskey and gin loosened lips, Loomis and Newell talked of going away together. Newell suffered from tuberculosis and contemplated moving to the more hospitable mountain climate of Colorado. The next morning, Loomis contacted the Colorado State Board of Medicine about obtaining a license to practice.

Investigators finally had the missing piece: a tangible motive. They envisioned a scenario in which Grace Loomis learned of her husband's clandestine meetings with G. On the evening of February 22, she confronted him. The argument turned violent and ended with Loomis bludgeoning her to death. This scenario, however, failed to explain that none of the witnesses within earshot of the Loomis house heard shouting or a male voice. The job of selling the case to a jury would fall to Prosecutor Robert Toms, who spent much of May and June grappling with Louis Colombo in court. On Tuesday, April 12, McNally and Navarre arrested Loomis for a second time at his office.

The Loomis trial became the hottest ticket in town. And the hardest to obtain. A *Free Press* reporter described the tidal wave of spectators who flooded into the courtroom when the bailiff opened the doors to the first day of testimony, Thursday, May 26, 1927: "The surge forward was overwhelming. Less than 100 persons can be seated in the court room, but fully 300 pressed in, those who had lost out in the fight for seats seemingly quite content, even happy, to stand, with not a fraction of an inch separating one from another."

They hoped to see the best show in town, a spectacle performed by "the other woman," contentious lawyers and, standing in the center of the melee, the cool-headed physician.

The *Detroit Times* sent reporter Lee J. Smits to cover the trial. Smits, a keen observer with an eye for detail, kept a close watch on Loomis. The perceptive journalist wrote a series documenting the human element of the trial—the dress of the key figures, their behavior on the stand, the tone of voice they used when testifying, the facial expressions of the jurors—which ran alongside hard news of the proceedings.

Loomis's apparent lack of emotion shocked the journalist, who described his subject's stoic demeanor. "His face is without color and his eyes are deeply shadowed, but he walks and stands and sits with no sign of strain." At one point, Smits tailed the embattled doctor into the hallway during a break in the courtroom action. "At recess he lights a cigarette and stands quietly in a corridor," Smits wrote, "and now then a slight, quick smile comes to his lips."

The smile intrigued Smits. "He spoke to a policeman, and smiled, during a rest in the ghastly proceedings," the reporter noted, "and he smiled politely over the matter of a chair out of place between the press table and the counsel table." Loomis's grin, which appeared to suggest a mix of disdain and amusement, became the defendant's defining characteristic. When the prosecution called Ethel Bell to the stand, he grinned as if following the cue of an invisible director.

Billed as the state's star witness, Ethel Bell claimed to have heard screams coming from the Loomis sunroom at five minutes before 9:00 p.m., which was five minutes before the defendant said he left for a stroll.

During his cross-examination, Colombo drove Ethel Bell to the point of a nervous breakdown with a series of relentless questions. In an attempt to discredit her testimony and shatter the timeline that the prosecution attempted to establish for the murder, Colombo scored points with the jury when he showed that the very attractive and very married twenty-five-year-old had stepped out on her husband that night with Charles Blockson.

Ethel Bell had little choice but to air her dirty laundry in court and admitted to a longstanding affair with the butcher. She explained to a titillated audience of seasoned court-goers that during the interval between the Loomis murder and the trial, she had divorced her husband and married Blockson.

After listening to Colombo's brutal cross-examination, Smits asked the question that Loomis's defense hoped to impose on the jurors: "Does a girl's romantic passion…and her later divorce and re-marriage, have any bearing on her capacity for telling the truth under oath?"

Eighteen-year-old telephone operator Dorothy McClure testified about the two calls she received from Garfield 0800, the Loomis residence, on the night of February 22. The first call came in sometime—she could not fix the exact time—between 7:00 p.m. and 8:42 p.m., when she took her fifteen-minute break. When she asked for a number, the woman on the other end of the line said, "Never mind."

McClure returned to her switchboard at 8:57 p.m. and received a second call from Garfield 0800 at 9:05 p.m. "Nobody answered but a scream," Doris testified. When Colombo asked her to imitate the scream, she demurred, instead describing it as "a lady's scream."

She explained the process she robotically followed in such circumstances. "You say 'Number, please?' Then you say 'Operator' twice and then you plug it permanent and plug the B operator." Doris plugged the Garfield 0800 call at 9:05 p.m. and retried the number at 9:06 p.m. It was dead.

An assistant city engineer testified about retracing the path of Loomis's fateful forty-five-minute stroll. After walking the route in thirty-five minutes, he concluded that there was a ten-minute gap in Loomis's timeline—a gap Toms hoped the jurors would see as a window in which the defendant returned home and surprised his wife in the sunroom.

Curiously, neither Toms nor Colombo included Gertrude Newell on his list of witnesses, probably because she could not damage or support

Loomis's alibi. It was an odd omission for Toms because Newell supposedly represented the only known motive in the case. In fact, detectives arrested Loomis when they discovered his relationship with Newell, so she was the catalyst for Loomis's second arrest. Yet if anything, Toms downplayed the doctor's illicit relationship with the attractive divorcée.

A *Detroit Times* reporter later explained this seemingly strange omission. "Inasmuch as she was considered a hostile witness to the State and because of the testimony of Dr. Loomis, Mrs. Newell could be used only as a rebuttal witness," the unnamed reporter wrote. "The prosecution therefore did not place her on the stand, although she was held for several weeks under heavy bail as a police witness against the physician."

Toms called a few witnesses who testified about the blood on Dr. Loomis's coat, but the state's case rested on the testimony of an eighteen-year-old telephone operator and a twenty-five-year-old on an illicit assignation with her lover. Their testimony established a timeframe for the murder as five minutes before Loomis supposedly left for his stroll.

Toms's case was thin. He failed to establish a compelling motive, the forensic scientists could not link Loomis to the crime scene with any physical evidence and the timeframe established for the murder did not implicate Loomis. After Toms finished questioning his final witness, Colombo made a motion to "direct a verdict of not guilty" on the grounds that the state had failed to make its case, but Judge John V. Brennan did not agree.

The trial really turned into a spectacle when Loomis took the stand in his own defense. Striding to the witness box wearing the overcoat stained with his wife's blood, Loomis shocked even habitual court-goers. Then, with Colombo acting the part of the slain Grace Loomis by lying on the floor in front of the jurors, Dr. Loomis reenacted finding his wife's body and feeling for her pulse—the sequence that caused the bloodstains on his overcoat but not the underlying shirt. Upon cross-examination by Toms, the defendant gave a repeat performance by replaying the moment.

During his time on the stand, Loomis repeated the same story he told police when they first questioned him. He also denied anything more than a friendship with Gertrude Newell.

After a trial that saw several weeks of testimony, the unexpected death of the thirteenth juror, the nervous breakdown of the court reporter and near breakdown of one of the witnesses (Ethel Bell) and another juror taken to a hospital for emergency treatment, the case went to the jury in late June. The trial circus ended when they returned a verdict of "not guilty."

The Loomis jury, the first in the history of Wayne County with a reserve or "thirteenth" juror. The thirteenth juror in the Loomis trial unexpectedly died during the proceedings. *Author's collection.*

After the trial, Dr. Loomis continued, even flaunted his affair with Gertrude Newell. They frequented the city's most notorious watering holes, in particular the Hungarian Café at West End and West Jefferson Avenues, and moved in together.

Speaking anonymously to the press in May 1928, a landlady who rented a house to the lovebirds described her tenants. Her statement about Loomis's flagging finances suggested that Newell's interest in the doctor was proportionate to the size of his bank accounts. "It seemed the worse Dr. Loomis's financial condition became," she said, "the more desire Mrs. Newell had to go out. He told me he could not afford the pace, but that he simply could not live without Gertrude so he would have to keep going 'until the end.'"

The landlady characterized Newell as suffering from "an insatiable craze" that left her "forever going" and Dr. Loomis as "insanely jealous." On several occasions, this mixture led to a volatile chemical reaction. "He raved and shouted when Mrs. Newell failed to come home at night," the landlady explained. On one occasion, he smashed some dishes. On another, he burned up a pair of underwear someone else had given to her.

Newell typically quieted Loomis's rants by threatening to take up with another man or return to her husband, and he responded with a profusion of apologies. She packed her bags and left after one particularly nasty rant. "Gertrude told me then," the woman explained, "that she was afraid to be alone with the doctor, because of his temper."

He apologized, she acquiesced and once again they moved in together. They shared an apartment in Richton Manor, living under the assumed names of "Mr. and Mrs. Brown," although by May 1928, Dr. Loomis had begun spending nights on a cot in his office.

By all accounts, the relationship was tumultuous. According to the building caretaker, one argument ended with Loomis kicking in the apartment door. Residents of their apartment building told of a shouting match that occurred on Friday, May 18, 1928.

The pitch of the argument grew so loud that their tête-à-tête became public. An upstairs neighbor who heard the argument through his floor recalled one specific, provocative statement. "I know as much about you as you know about me," "Mrs. Brown" screeched. Then the apartment door slammed.

Loomis stormed out of the building and went to his office, located in a building on Grand River Avenue. The arguments, it later emerged, resulted because "Mrs. Brown" wanted "Mr. Brown" to marry her and he refused because he began to question her faithfulness. She reportedly taunted Loomis with statements such as "Why don't you be big and strong like other men?"

The office became a sanctuary of sorts, although by May 19 he stood on the verge of losing it. Beginning with his acquittal, Dr. Loomis's life began a downward spiral that reached its nadir in the spring of 1928. One by one, his patients defected to other, less notorious physicians. Everywhere he turned, people looked at him and whispered. He received threatening phone calls at all hours. By May 1928, he had become a refugee sleeping in his office, which he could no longer afford. He worried about the money needed to support Frank Jr. and Jeanette, who lived with relatives in Brooklyn.

On May 19, 1928—a year after the murder trial made daily headlines—a janitor in Loomis's office building discovered the doctor unconscious on the couch in a fellow physician's office. A rubber tube inserted into his mouth ran to a pump that had discharged a lethal dose of gas.

Before Loomis turned on the gas, he wrote two suicide notes, one intended for the press and the other addressed to his friend Victor Kolar, the assistant director of the Detroit Symphony Orchestra. He enclosed the two notes in an unsealed envelope and left it in the appointment book of his colleague Dr. C.J. Kirwin along with directions to send one of the notes to the press and the other to Kolar.

Then Loomis scribbled a third note. Addressed to "The Detroit Police Department," the note hinted at a forthcoming revelation: "A newspaper article will be published in 24 or 48 hours explaining this action on my part. Please be patient until then." It was signed "Dr. F.R. Loomis."

Dr. Kirwin discovered the envelopes later that day and, after consulting with fellow physicians, decided to follow Loomis's directions to the letter. The note earmarked for publication went to the *Detroit News*, and the other note went to Victor Kolar.

Any hopes for a deathbed confession died when the *Detroit News* published Dr. Loomis's suicide note, dated May 19, 1928. Instead, he indicted Robert Toms for grandstanding during the trial ("political maneuvering on the part of would-be office holders"; Toms later became "Judge Toms") and the newspapers for running inaccurate stories about his case.

> *I am not guilty of murder.*
>
> *My conscious* [sic] *is clear.*
>
> *I have endured to my mind the severest kind of humiliation, and disrespect, for over a year.*
>
> *This was all due to cheap political maneuvering on the part of would-be office holders.*
>
> *My trouble now is terrible loneliness and disrespect and discouragement.*
>
> *I have done things for which I have been most cruelly criticized. What I have done I am proud of, and consider my actions as a duty attempted.*
>
> *The public many times reads things in the paper which are untrue. Before my trial I was also guilty of swallowing newspaper articles whole, so I don't entirely blame readers of believing things at their first glance at the paper.*
>
> *Many have never learned the lesson which I have had. So long as the paper continues to print articles which they know to be untrue, just so long many innocent people will have to suffer along with those whom the paper is trying originally to hurt.*
>
> *I have many wonderful friends both in Detroit and Brooklyn, Mich., where I grew to be a man. All these people and patients I wish to thank now from the bottom of my heart.*
>
> *I am proud that my life was such as to merit (I believe) such a wonderful friendship.*
>
> *Please print this in the paper just as it stands.*
>
> *DR. F.R. LOOMIS*

Following the publication of Loomis's suicide note, Gertrude Newell once again became a front-page starlet. To both the police and the press, she downplayed the troubles that afflicted their relationship. "We were the best of friends, right up to the end," she said. "Reports by the police department that we had quarreled and that he had threatened me are absolutely false. I had no intention of deserting him."

After wrestling with his conscience, which he said involved fifty sleepless hours, Victor Kolar decided to go public with the letter Loomis had addressed to him. It appears that Loomis intended the note for Kolar's eyes only, but Kolar turned it over to the police. Eventually, the note made its way into the papers.

> *Mr. Kolar:*
>
> *I want to express my appreciation to you for our friendship. It was a bright spot in my life.*
>
> *G. drives me crazy. Everyone in Detroit should receive consideration but myself.*
>
> *She was home when I arrived. Her father let her come in alone on the interurban at 11:30 p.m. When I expressed myself in regard to his letting her take such a trip alone at night she upheld him and told me she was going to Ypsi to live with him. Of course I used my tongue to no good advantage as usual.*
>
> *My God! How I love her! Perhaps we will meet again when both of us will be more reasonable.*
>
> *Good-bye to you.*
>
> *I appreciate so much for all you have tried to do for G. and I. Protect her all you can.*
>
> *With the kindest regards to you both, and may happiness be yours to the fullest. Bid G. good-bye for me and tell her I love her.*
>
>   *F.*
>
> *If anything should happen to G., Mr. Kolar, in the near future, try to have her placed in my grave.*
>
>   *F.*

The Kolar letter created an additional complication for Gertrude Newell, whose denials about a screaming match on May 18 now appeared suspect. Investigators also wondered if the line "If anything should happen to G," indicated that "Mr. and Mrs. Brown" had entered into a suicide pact. The overheard snippet of argument in which "Mrs. Brown" alluded to knowing something about "Mr. Brown"—"I know as much about you as you know about me"—convinced Frahm that Newell knew something about the Grace Loomis murder and possibly even had guilty knowledge.

When Frahm went to interview Newell after learning about the Kolar letter, he found her on the verge of a total breakdown, unhinged by the media storm that resulted in her portrait once again looming large on the front pages of every rag in the city. She had left the Brown apartment and taken refuge at the Seville Hotel, where she remained a shut-in for several days after her lover's suicide.

Even Frahm, the tough-as-nails detective hardened by years on the prowl, did not want to be responsible for Newell's further unraveling. "I shall not ask her any questions regarding Dr. Loomis's suicide," he said, "but I want officially to give her an opportunity to make any sort of statement she cares to give out. Then I am through."

For Frahm, the case ended with Dr. Loomis's suicide, which doubled as the doctor's confession despite the bold denial ("I am not guilty of murder") in the first line of the physician's suicide note.

"I believed Dr. Loomis to be innocent when I defended him, and I still believe that he is innocent," attorney Louis J. Colombo remarked following the suicide of his most infamous client. "He was a victim of police persecution. I have never known a braver man than Dr. Loomis." Loomis never wavered in his story or in his innocence, Colombo pointed out, even though he was protected from further prosecution by the doctrine of double jeopardy.

In a testament to the tremendous notoriety of the Loomis case, Detroit police legend Fred Frahm listed it among the city's most infamous unsolved murders when interviewed by *Free Press* reporter C.G. Givens for an article published in August 1928. Frahm, with typical braggadocio, claimed to possess a "little black book" labeled "Past Due Accounts." The ledger contained "secret reports of the homicide squad to its chief, Fred Frahm," and in them solutions to the most vexing cold cases in the city's history. Yet Frahm knew that it wasn't a matter of knowing whodunit, but proving it.

"I have some letters here which might throw a whole lot of light on the Loomis case," Frahm said. "These letters, of course, cannot be quoted. But strange as it may sound, the murderer of Mrs. Loomis left many an open clew [*sic*]—his crime was not nearly so secretly accomplished as he might have believed. I have this letter here—and had it been possible to have forced the woman who wrote it to testify, the murderer of Mrs. Loomis might now have been in prison." Frahm was as vague about the identity of this secret witness as about the content of the smoking-gun letters.

One possible author of Frahm's mystery letters may have been an anonymous witness who contacted the police shortly after the murder. The woman refused to come forward but claimed to have walked past the Loomis residence during the murder. Through the gap of the partially closed blind, she claimed to have seen both the murder and the murderer. Pregnant and terrified, she refused to come forward, which would explain Frahm's remark about forcing "the woman who wrote it to testify."

When Givens asked Frahm if he still considered the unsolved Grace Loomis murder and the "Greatrex baby" disappearance mysteries, the chief of detectives gave an enigmatic reply. They were still "mysteries to the public," he said. "But to the Little Black Book they are not mysteries. Only cases in which the culprits have not yet been convicted."

If it in fact existed, perhaps Frahm's "little black book," which he touted as worth millions to the criminal outfits of Prohibition-era Detroit, contains the solution to one of the most baffling cold cases in the city's storied history of crime.

Loomis investigator John Navarre was less enigmatic than Frahm and not only believed that Loomis did it but also that he gave a partial confession of sorts. In an exclusive interview with writer Lee J. Smits, the *Times* reporter who covered the Loomis trial, Navarre cited one of Loomis's statements that he believed represented a confession.

Shortly after Loomis's arrest and just prior to Loomis's hiring Colombo as his attorney, Navarre explained the difference between first-degree murder and manslaughter to his suspect. The detective pointed out that if Loomis killed his wife during a violent argument, he likely committed manslaughter.

"Now, doctor, don't you want to clear your mind once and for all of this terrible affair?" he asked. "You will feel better if you do."

Loomis thought for a moment and then replied, "Give me a little time to think it over, will you?" Then along came Colombo and the writ of habeas corpus. Later, during a break in the trial, Navarre approached Loomis outside of the courtroom and reminded him of this conversation. "Doctor, what about the matter we were discussing?"

And Loomis responded, "You'll have to talk with my lawyer."

Navarre believed that Loomis had thought about it, his answer coming on the morning of May 19, 1928. The suicide note, in which he proclaimed, "I am not guilty of murder," could be read as "I am guilty of manslaughter."

"He was not guilty of murder, technically, and he knew it," Navarre explained. "He was guilty of manslaughter. The natural expression would have been, 'I did not kill my wife,' or something of the sort, but Loomis used a legal phrase."

Navarre also had a theory about the murder weapon, which some investigators believed went into the furnace. "Dr. Albert French and I searched the premises for a weapon," Navarre explained. "We found none. But in the basement we found a number of sections of two-by-four that had been sharpened for use as stakes for a wire enclosure when Loomis was sodding his lawn. We stretched out the wire and assembled the stakes. There was one missing. Loomis first struck his wife with his fist, then went to the basement and got a two-by-four, with which he struck her three times on the back of the head, causing fatal concussion of the brain. Then he threw his stained shirt and the two-by-four into the blazing furnace."

As convincing as Navarre's theory sounds, it contains a troubling contradiction. If Loomis walloped his wife in the heat of an argument, then he would have more likely used something at hand as a weapon—like the telephone—instead of running to the basement. Unless, of course, he just happened to have a fence picket in hand when he walloped his wife. If he went to the basement for a wooden stake, perhaps because he wanted a wooden object that he could burn, then how did this constitute manslaughter?

If Loomis had not envisioned the crime ahead of time, then he possessed a surreal combination of an uncanny, almost superhuman ability to think under pressure and extraordinarily good luck. In the span of a few minutes, he stoked the furnace, destroyed the murder weapon and incriminating articles of clothing and managed to tiptoe out of the house unseen by any of the witnesses who heard suspicious screams just minutes earlier.

A *Free Press* reporter wrote a fitting coda to the mystery of Grace Loomis's murder in a piece that appeared after the doctor's suicide. "So far as was known, and so far as has ever been learned, a lone canary bird in a cage in the sun-room, was the only living witness to Mrs. Loomis' death."

And the canary didn't talk.

4

The St. Aubin Avenue
House of Horrors

(Detroit, 1929)

Today, nothing remains of the St. Aubin House of Horrors except an empty, overgrown lot and endless speculation about what happened there one dark morning in 1929. But for weeks after the murders, curious passersby paused in front of the house at 3587 St. Aubin Avenue and shuddered as they gazed at the boarded-up door. Two uniformed police officers kept a twenty-four-hour vigil over the front and back doors, preventing anyone from sneaking into the house and making off with a memento mori. The number of visitors decreased with each passing week until the story faded from memory and became part of Motor City folklore.

The macabre scene inside the Evangelist home on Wednesday, July 3, 1929, haunted detectives, even those seasoned by a decade of gangland violence in Prohibition-era Detroit, with nightmares of axe-wielding papier-mâché idols. Headline stories about the case, which involved the tangled web woven by a religious cult messiah and self-proclaimed faith healer, alternately captivated and horrified readers, supposedly causing one woman to throw herself out of the window of a downtown high-rise.

Just before noon on Wednesday, July 3, 1929, Vincent Elias dropped by to see his real estate partner, Benny Evangelist. The Evangelist family of six lived in a simple, box-like two-story house at 3587 St. Aubin Avenue in the heart of Detroit's "Little Italy." The residence also served as the epicenter of Evangelist's pseudo-Christian religion. Well known throughout the neighborhood as a cult messiah who claimed to have divine healing abilities, the family patriarch conducted religious ceremonies in his basement.

In Evangelist's office, Elias found a scene so revolting, he backtracked out of the house and made a beeline to the nearest police station. A squad of homicide detectives returned to the house with the shaken man in tow.

Benny Evangelist's headless body sat slumped in his desk chair with his severed head on the floor beside him. A single blow—inflicted with a razor-sharp knife or axe—came down on Evangelist's neck at such an angle and with such force that it took off his head in one swoop. The arterial spray from his neck splashed the wall above the desk and created a pool of blood around the body.

A line of bloody footprints led from Evangelist's office through the kitchen to the upstairs bedroom. Evangelist's wife, thirty-eight-year-old Santina, lay across the bed with eighteen-month-old Mario nestled by her side, his battered and bloody head resting in a crook of his mother's arm. They had apparently been asleep when their attacker tiptoed into the room carrying the blood-streaked weapon—an axe, machete or banana knife—used to behead the head of the family. Santina, perhaps alerted by the sound of creaking floorboards, apparently sat up or attempted to crawl out of bed when she noticed a silhouette leaning over her.

Standing over the slumbering woman, the assailant brought the heavy blade down on Santina's head and neck with such force that it severed muscle, tendons, ligaments and vertebrae, leaving her head connected to her torso by a few sinews and dangling over the side of the bed. Then he turned on the child.

The attack occurred so quickly and with such ferocity that the victims had no time to cry out. Anyone awake down the hall would have heard only a dull thud, like the sound of an axe biting into a tree trunk.

Blood was everywhere. The first blow opened a gash in Santina's scalp. When the slayer swung the weapon backward, flecks of blood peppered the ceiling. Each succeeding strike left more droplets. When the attack ended, the ceiling above the bed was covered with a crimson polka dot–like pattern. Lines of arterial spray streaked the wall beside the bed, and blood drenched the bedsheets and Santina's nightgown.

The morbid tableau continued in the adjacent bedroom, where the other three Evangelist children slept. Five-year-old Matthew lay across one of the twin beds. (His facial features were so battered, police assumed he was a

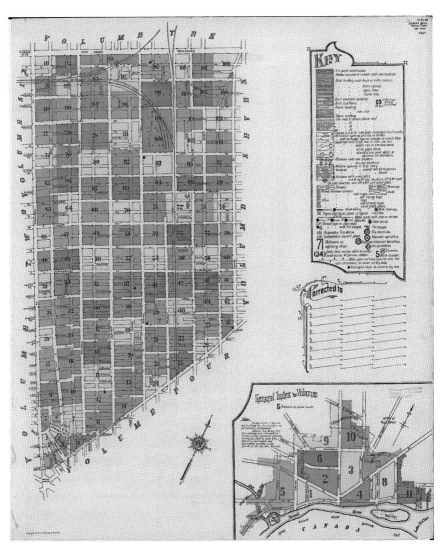

A 1921 Sanborn Fire Insurance Map showing the area of Detroit framed by Woodward Avenue, East Grand Boulevard, Grandy Avenue and Gratiot Avenue. St. Aubin Avenue begins between blocks 25 and 26 and runs north. *Library of Congress Geography and Map Division.*

female until the autopsy verified his sex. Contemporary news reports errantly referred to him as "Margaret.") His four-year-old sister, Eugenia, was the other. The oldest Evangelist daughter, seven-year-old Evangeline (also called "Angeline"), lay on the floorboards by the door leading to a porch. All three had been hacked to death.

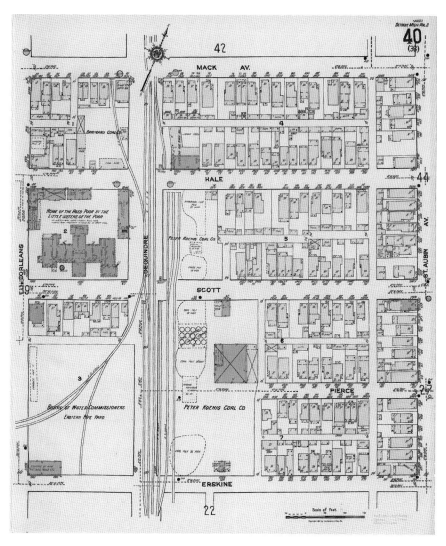

A close-up showing a portion of "Little Italy." The Evangelist family lived at 3587 St. Aubin Avenue, located at the upper right corner of the map. *Library of Congress Geography and Map Division.*

Deep incisions in the shoulders, inflicted after death, hinted at the possibility that the killer had attempted to sever his victims' arms. The sheer savageness of the crime scene inspired Wayne County deputy coroner George Berg to declare, "These are the worst murders I've ever seen in all my years of coroner's work."

The basement contained the epicenter of Benny Evangelist's religious cult: a cellar sanctuary lined in green cloth and populated by wax figures with oversized papier-mâché heads. The idols, suspended from the ceiling by steel wires, sported goggle-like eyes and such realistic features as arm hair, which came from Evangelist's pet Airedale and German Shepherds, and wigs fashioned from real human hair. In the center of the grotesque menagerie dangled a giant eyeball illuminated by an electric light that Evangelist referred to as "the sun." In this so-called séance room, he preached to followers of his Union Federation of America and, according to some accounts, whipped his followers into a frenzy. The figures—the "celestial prophets"—may have been personifications of "celestial" planets; a sign in the basement window advertised "Great Celestial Planet Exhibition."

Amid the religious paraphernalia was the centerpiece of Evangelist's religion: a three-hundred-page tome titled *The Oldest History of the World Discovered by Occult Science in Detroit, Mich.* This gospel according to Benedict Evangelist contained the sermons he used to transfix his followers—estimated at anywhere from three hundred to three thousand in number—in his cellar ceremonies.

A who's who of Detroit investigators viewed the scene—including Chief of Detectives Edward H. Fox, acting head of the homicide squad Detective Lieutenant John Navarre and fingerprint expert Charles S. Carmody—while a cordon of uniformed cops held back the throng of curious onlookers who wanted nothing more than a glimpse at the scene of the crime.

The investigators quickly linked the murders to Evangelist's cult and formed the working theory that religious mania inspired the slaughter.

Lieutenant Royal A. Baker, the department's so-called in-house expert on "criminal degeneracy" and Prohibition-era Detroit's version of a criminal profiler, concluded that the mentally unbalanced killer may have wiped out the Evangelist family to please the wax- and papier-mâché gods in the cellar. Baker also posited that the killer might have come to Evangelist for spiritual healing. When introduced to the idols in "the séance room," the unknown perpetrator became convinced that Evangelist used them to conjure evil spirits and subsequently murdered the "divine prophet" and his entire family to prevent these black masses.

The crime scene yielded some provocative clues. The desk contained bits and pieces of Evangelist's two lives. Mundane personal items, such as a sheaf of letters in Italian, represented Benny Evangelist the man. Spiritual trinkets represented Benny Evangelist, the "divine prophet" and faith healer. A smattering of business cards—some advertising Evangelist's worldly profession as a carpenter and real estate agent, others hawking his spiritual line of faith healing—provided a visible reminder of this duality.

The business cards strewn across Evangelist's desk told the story of his two professions. One set of cards advertised his services as a real estate contractor, which included property transactions as well as building and repair. A second set of cards advertised his services as a self-proclaimed messiah and faith healer: "Mr. Benny Evangelist, divine profetil, author and private history writer." A carpenter by trade, Evangelist had recently sold his carpentry shop because his second business had become lucrative enough to support his family.

Evangelist's office contained a potpourri of religious paraphernalia that represented an eclectic mixture of Christianity and his own cult practices. A picture of the Last Supper and a crucifix sat beside a wig and fake beard that he may have worn during his "readings," healings and ceremonies. A photograph of a child in a coffin, which would turn out to be one of the most provocative and most enigmatic clues found in the home, was lying on the floorboards.

The lamp on the desk was still on when Vincent Elias found Benny Evangelist's decapitated body slumped in his desk chair, which suggested a likely timeframe for the crime.

According to the Wayne County medical examiner, the murders took place approximately eight hours earlier, which put them sometime between midnight and 3:00 a.m. on the morning of July 3. Circumstantial evidence corroborated this finding. During that interval, Evangelist told his followers, he communed with spirits and communicated with the moon and the clouds. The killer evidently tiptoed behind Evangelist while he was entranced and struck him during his nightly communion with the clouds, which suggested that the killer knew about Evangelist's rituals and possibly belonged to his cult.

The angle of the wounds indicated a left-handed killer, who left behind a series of bloody shoe prints and two bloody fingerprints on the inside latch of the front door. The print on the door latch came from the killer's right hand, which led to the conclusion that a left-handed killer would have carried the murder weapon in his dominant hand and opened the door with his non-dominant right hand. The shoe prints were very small.

The office also contained a cache of women's lingerie and underwear, each tagged with the owner's name, which raised eyebrows among investigators but would later prove to be a red herring in the case.

Benjamino Evangelista emigrated from Italy in 1903 and changed his name to the Americanized "Benny Evangelist." In Philadelphia, Pennsylvania, he founded the Union Federation of America and began work on the first volume in what appeared to be a four-volume bible. Supposedly, Evangelist conceived of the bible while in trances that occurred between midnight and 3:00 a.m. According to *The Oldest History of the World*, it was during this time when the "celestial bodies" became visible to him. Apparently, he dictated his visions to a ghostwriter who produced the text. Although police searched high and low for Evangelist's collaborator, they never managed to identify him.

"My story is from my own views and signs that I see from 12 to 3 a.m.," Evangelist wrote. "I began on February 2, 1906 in Philadelphia, Pa., and it was completed on February 2, 1926, in the city of Detroit, County of Wayne, State of Michigan. On this new earth, the last one was created by God, the Father Celestial and the great Prophet Miel. We call it today the great Union Federation of America. I am with the power of God and I respect this nation. In this book I shall express all my views of the past 20 years. In this great continent we are all the generations." Ominously, Evangelist noted in the preface to *The Oldest History* that he planned on writing three additional volumes if "he lived."

Evangelist's bible contained, among other re-imaginings of Old Testament stories, a new twist on the story of Adam and Eve in the Garden of Eden. "Eve was troubled and went to ask Eldom's advice," he wrote. "Eldom said it was something you had eaten that disturbed you, and Eve believed what he had told her. The serpents were very happy in the thought they were getting revenge on Eve."

The bible-according-to-Evangelist contained some interesting scenes that had detectives contemplating if life had imitated art on St. Aubin Avenue. In one scene, a character tears the head off another character and tosses it at the victim's feet. In other scenes, various characters have their arms wrenched from their torsos. Just as the killer had known when Evangelist communed with the planets, he had known about the grisly fates of Evangelist's biblical characters. This further convinced detectives that Evangelist's killer was a member of his cult.

In addition to leading prayer ceremonies, Benny Evangelist also—for a fee of ten dollars—offered private readings during which he healed the various afflictions of his followers. He administered "love potions" and other remedies concocted from various combinations of herbs and spices that he grew in his backyard garden.

A neighbor who brought her sick child to Evangelist for treatment described the process:

> He told Michael to sit down opposite him. Then he read something from a book, or a piece of paper. I don't know what it was. It was neither English nor Italian. He read for about fifteen minutes, and then made the sign of the cross on the little boy's forehead. Then he sat quietly for a minute with his hands in his lap and his eyes closed. Then he rubbed his fingers over the boy's forehead again and told us to go home—that little Michael would get well.

And little Michael did get well, which went a long way in increasing the divine profetil's street credibility. This sideline apparently became quite a moneymaker for Evangelist, known throughout Detroit's Little Italy as "Benny the healer." Just before the murders, he purchased a farm about fifty miles from Detroit on which he planned to build a summer home for his family. Nonetheless, according to neighbors, Evangelist always seemed short of money.

Although Evangelist founded a cult and positioned himself at its head as divine prophet, he never completely strayed from the Catholic Church. He regularly attended Sunday mass at the San Francesco Catholic Church at the corner of Rivard and Brewster.

Father Francis Beccherini, who came to know the "divine prophet" well, described Evangelist as "insane" but nevertheless a successful venture capitalist whose venture—the cult—had made him quite a bit of capital. Beccherini, however, dismissed Evangelist's cult as nothing more than a moneymaking venture with Evangelist as a manipulative Svengali, a twisted ringmaster directing the circus.

"I do not believe Evangelist was sincere in practicing the creed he established," Father Beccherini said on the eve of presiding over the family's funeral. "Rather, I believe he founded the mysterious cult, with all of its weird props and practices, with the sole idea of making money. His was a practical mind."

Beccherini, who baptized all of the Evangelist children, characterized both Benny and Santina Evangelist as religious fanatics. Although they followed established church traditions, such as the rite of baptism, they constantly pestered their parish priest with tales of their ability to conjure demons from the nether world. Unimpressed and undaunted, Beccherini dismissed them and instructed parish helpers to stay away from the couple in order to avoid any potential scandal.

Police headquarters resembled a busy anthill on the night of Thursday, July 3. Detectives, led by John I. Navarre of the Homicide Squad, brought in any and every friend, acquaintance and associate of Benny Evangelist with the hopes that someone knew something.

Vincent Elias, who the day before had stumbled into one of the bloodiest crime scenes in the city's storied history, spent some time in an interrogation room trying to persuade detectives that the shoe didn't fit. Because his shoe size corresponded with the bloody footprint found at the scene, Elias had to convince detectives that he did not make them, which he managed to accomplish after a few tense hours.

Evangelist's lawyer Anthony A. Esperi told of numerous court actions involving the real estate guru, mostly over minor affairs, like the collection of land contract payments, none of which generated the type of animosity that might have led to the massacre.

On the contrary, people either liked Evangelist or viewed him as a harmless crackpot known for his sidewalk preaching—animated events in which he often spread his arms wide and gazed at the sky. He guarded his cellar shrine and rarely allowed outsiders to see the "celestial prophets" until about a month before his demise, when he staged an exhibition in the basement.

When not in the public eye, Benny had a sharper edge. According to those most familiar with the family, he had a quick temper that led to periodic verbal sparring with his wife. Benny apparently liked his wife to play a passive, subservient role, and when she sassed him or talked back to him, he railed at her. Their verbal sparring, however, never progressed to physical sparring, and never did she even contemplate leaving him.

Evangelist's doctor, Alf Thomas, said that Benny and Santina had not been married for long. He believed the four children were Santina's from another marriage. Dr. Thomas described Evangelist as insane, his delusions of grandeur evident in his scheme to make a motion picture that he believed would bring his teachings to a wider audience.

A *Detroit Free Press* staff writer agreed, characterizing the prophet as "hopelessly mad on the subject of the cult on which he was the leader." Hopelessly mad or not, Benny Evangelist managed to gather a substantially large flock, the true number of whom would remain unknown because no cult followers came forward during the investigation. Not one. After the unidentified murderer cut off the head of the cult, it appeared, the body simply withered and died.

Navarre's men immediately identified two known associates of Evangelist's as persons of interest. Angelo Depoli and Umberto Tecchio shared a room at a nearby boardinghouse, both knew Evangelist and Tecchio was one of the last people to see Evangelist alive.

Angelo Depoli became a convenient suspect when a quick sweep of the rooming house barn uncovered an axe, a banana knife and a newly washed pair of shoes. Dragged in for questioning, Depoli admitted he knew the Evangelist family but denied any involvement with the murders. Forensic examination of the axe—old, rusty and barely carrying an edge—and the banana knife indicated that they had not been used in the murders.

Like Depoli, Umberto Tecchio admitted knowing Evangelist. He once brought his wife to Benny the healer for treatment. Furthermore, Evangelist owned the paper on Umberto Tecchio's house, and the two men had some type of heated exchange in Evangelist's office at approximately 8:00 p.m.—just a few hours before the murders—when Tecchio dropped by to make a final payment on his mortgage. Camillo Tress, who roomed at the same boardinghouse as Tecchio (the two men shared two halves of a room separated by a bedsheet used as a makeshift wall), went with Tecchio but waited on the front porch. Tress said he could not hear what the two men said to each other but recalled that Tecchio's voice sounded elevated, almost angry, although he shrugged this off as the high-pitched tone Tecchio typically used when talking.

All of a sudden, the minor legal disputes that Evangelist's lawyer described took on a new, sinister significance as Tecchio's possible motive. Tecchio said that he had stopped by Evangelist's house to make a final house payment, but detectives found the deed among the boxes of papers they carted off to police headquarters. If Tecchio had made the payment, as he said, then Evangelist would have given him the paper.

Umberto Tecchio also had a temper. This propensity for violence was evident in an incident that had occurred three months before the Evangelist murders. On April 19, 1929, he stabbed his brother-in-law Bart Maffio to death over a dispute involving a debt. Tecchio sidestepped charges when investigators concluded that he had acted in self-defense. His wife was less understanding and even less forgiving. Three weeks after Tecchio murdered her brother, she divorced him.

At first, detectives considered Tecchio a prime suspect in the Evangelist case, but their suspicions crumbled under the weight of a rock-solid alibi. He left Evangelist's house and went straight to the boardinghouse, arriving shortly after 8:00 p.m. After changing clothes, he and Tress went to several blind pigs and wobbled back to the boardinghouse at around 11:00 p.m., where he stayed for the remainder of the night. Tecchio's alibi checked out. At the time an unknown assailant reddened his hatchet at 3587 St. Aubin Avenue, Umberto Tecchio slumbered in a house at 2630 Pierce Street. Acting on a hot telephone tip, detectives also brought in Sam Verecchia, John Valentine and Steve Azzoli, all of whom knew Evangelist and none of whom knew a thing about the murders.

The forensic evidence found at the crime scene exonerated all five men. Their get-out-of-jail card came in the form of a fingerprint card; reportedly, none of their fingerprints matched the bloody fingerprints lifted from the door latch, although the clarity of the print became a hotly debated topic among those in the know (which did not include reporters). Verecchia, Valentine and Azzoli left police headquarters almost immediately, while detectives decided to hold on to Depoli and Tecchio with the hope that they knew something that might help with the investigation.

Marie Pasici, an attractive twenty-nine-year-old brunette, joined the parade of Evangelist acquaintances shuffling into and out of police headquarters. She became a person of interest simply because she happened to stop by the house of horrors on the afternoon of July 3 and appeared interested in what had happened. A brief interrogation revealed that Marie's husband, whom she described as "sick in the head," had undergone "treatments" by Evangelist and she had come by the house to pick up his "prescription."

Mrs. Bernard Saurine, a close friend of the Evangelist family, gushed about Benny the healer's uncanny ability to cure both physical and spiritual afflictions. "Time after time, Benny effected wonderful cures," she told an astonished *Detroit Times* reporter. "He was well known all over the country for his healing, and many people came to him from other cities. Of course," she admitted, "he did not always cure, but in the majority of cases I think he did."

"Benny the healer," she said, originally met Santina when she came to him for help. She described the herbal courtship of Evangelist and his patient. Soon after arriving in Detroit from southern Italy, she became ill. "A friend heard of Benny and four men carried her to Benny's home for a treatment."

Apparently smitten, Benny charged Santina a bit more than his usual ten-dollar fee. The upcharge included wedding vows. "'I can cure you,' he said, 'but you must marry me.'" She agreed, Benny healed her, and, making good on her promise, Santina became Mrs. Evangelist.

At first, detectives wondered if the women's lingerie and underwear hinted that Evangelist practiced some sort of black magic or "Voodooism." At the time, it was widely believed that a voodoo practitioner could find a missing person through a piece of clothing. Then, a more earthy explanation emerged; perhaps the lingerie represented payment for healing services rendered. This explanation provided another possible motive: a jealous husband, cuckolded by the charismatic Evangelist, sought revenge by wiping out the homewrecker's entire family.

The Saurines' son C.D. provided an innocent explanation for the apparel found in the Evangelist house. Benny the healer, he explained, required a piece of clothing to execute the healing process for those who could not meet with him in person, and the article of attire had to have been worn close to the body. Saurine dismissed any salaciousness. "You would find lots of lingerie and men's underwear and night clothing in any healer's house."

Detectives began to wonder if one of the healer's less successful "treatments" had motived his murderer. One theory that emerged involved a revenge killing by either an unsatisfied client or someone connected with an unsatisfied client. They based this line of inquiry on the photograph found on the floor of Evangelist's office.

The little boy in the photograph appeared sleeping, but the size and shape of the box, the attire and expressions worn by others in the photograph were dead giveaways that this was a funereal scene. Found on the floor by Evangelist's decollated corpse and not far from his disembodied head, the photograph may have had some symbolic significance in the crime. Detectives followed a line that the little boy represented one of Evangelist's unsuccessful healing attempts. Aggrieved, the boy's father decided to seek vengeance not with a lawyer or a police officer but with an axe. The only clue on the photograph came in the form of a photographer's stamp on the reverse.

Navarre sent detectives to find the photographer. He hoped that the photographer's files would reveal a name. Like the other leads in the Evangelist investigation, however, it turned into a dead end when the boy turned out to be one of the Evangelist children, who died five years earlier, in 1924.

Navarre's team also explored the possible connection between the slaughter of the Evangelist family and the frenzied attack on a family of four in River Rouge two weeks earlier. The River Rouge police chief theorized that the Cipinski killer may have communed with "the divine prophet" and, fearing that Evangelist might talk, iced him and his entire family.

According to a *Detroit Times* reporter, however, police investigating the Evangelist crime "placed little credence" in the theory that the same axman murdered both families. "While both of the wholesale murders were committed somewhat similarly," he wrote, "they are thought to have been born of different motives."

Detroit authorities, in fact, treated the possible connection between the Cipinski and Evangelist families as a serious line of inquiry. But when a comparison of fingerprints lifted at the River Rouge crime scene and the bloody prints taken from the front door of the Detroit crime scene did not match, they dismissed any remaining similarities between the two cases as pure coincidence.

News of the St. Aubin Avenue massacre hit the streets on July 4, 1929. The headline of the *Detroit Free Press* page-one story stretched from margin to margin: "POLICE JAIL FRIEND OF VICTIMS IN AX KILLINGS OF SIX IN CULT HOME." The *Detroit Times* ran an even larger headline: "FIVE HELD IN AX SLAYINGS." The *Free Press* correspondent wrote, "Behind the tragedy was a grotesque background of religious insanity paralleling in its weirdness and barbarism [of] any voodoo fetish of the West Indies."

One reader became so unnerved by news of the cult murders she threw herself out the window of a downtown high-rise. Like many Detroiters, thirty-six-year-old Florence Morris found herself captivated—and horrified—by the Evangelist murders. The killings hit a little too close to home, however, and irrational fears over the safety of her own four children began to consume her. She convinced herself that an axe wielded by some faceless demon would come down on her and her children.

On Saturday, July 6, a frantic Mrs. Morris went to police headquarters and demanded protection for her children. Policewomen attempted to calm the frightened woman and called her husband, who took her home and tried in vain to convince his wife that she and their children were in no danger. Three hours later, Florence Morris jumped from the forty-two-story Barnum tower. She plummeted twenty-three stories onto the brick pavement of the alley behind the Barnum and died on impact.

Another Detroiter who became entranced by the unsolved cult murders, a self-proclaimed astrologist named Clark Robson, found a partial solution in the stars. After studying the positions of the planets on the day of Benny Evangelist's birth as well as the morning of the murders, Robson came up with a stunningly specific astro-profile of the killer: short in height with a wiry build, dark complexion, reddish-tinged hair and an eccentric personality. Robson thought the killer had a female accomplice and killed out of jealousy. According to Robson's horoscope, the perpetrator, who knew Evangelist well, enjoyed bragging about his exploits, and his loose lips would probably lead to his discovery. If he failed to give himself away accidentally, then he might give himself away deliberately by surrendering to police, so he could bask in the vainglory of his crimes. Police would not need to find the killer, Robson said; the killer would find them.

By this time, Lieutenant Royal A. Baker—who initially theorized that the killer was a delusional maniac who murdered the Evangelist family to placate the gods in the basement—had come up with an alternate profile. A sadist, the perpetrator murdered the family because he enjoyed watching them suffer. Such an individual, Baker reasoned, had killed before and had become desensitized to violence and therefore had to kill an entire family to satisfy his bloodlust. Baker believed that the killer would strike again, possibly another family but in a city other than Detroit.

While detectives worked around the clock chasing down leads all over Detroit, the bodies of the six Evangelists lay in state at the undertaking establishment of F.J. Calcaterra. An estimated wave of six to eight thousand neighbors, friends and morbid curiosity-seekers stood in a line that stretched around the block and attempted to fan away the intense heat while they waited for their turn to shuffle past the line of coffins. Many of them blanched at the sight of the slain children.

On Saturday, July 6, all of the key players from the Detroit Police Department converged on the San Francesco Church, joining the throng of curious spectators cramming the pews to watch Father Beccherini's sendoff to the six-member Evangelist family. Most in the crowd came for some cheap, maudlin entertainment, but detectives hoped that the killer or killers also came to admire his handiwork. Detectives from the homicide and Black Hand departments and the amateur detectives who pulled themselves out of their easy chairs scanned faces in the crowd in the hopes of finding some clue that would expose the culprit. Because investigators envisioned a man with a wrestler's physique as their prime suspect, every short, broad-shouldered, heavy-set man with a small shoe size came under particular scrutiny.

The three thousand spectators milling about the church experienced a Keystone Cops–type scene when detectives arrested a ninety-pound weakling. The suspect, who rode his bicycle to the funeral, wore a tattered suit and an old straw hat. Navarre's boys handcuffed the startled spectator, escorted him to police headquarters and released him a few hours later when it became evident that they had nabbed the wrong man. Desperate to close the case, they were grasping at straw hats.

After five days of intense investigation, Navarre admitted that his team had gotten nowhere. Then, detectives received a confession of sorts in the form of an anonymous letter signed by "The Murderer."

> *My consions* [sic] *bother me since I killed that family of six so will confess and say I am sorry. I live on Lincoln avenue, in the 5400 block, but I won't give the house number because I want thinking time. Search the houses and you will find the bloody hatchet in a suitcase. I am ready for the worst punishment I can get.*

A team went door-knocking and searched houses, as the letter writer suggested, but failed to find a suitcase containing a blood-streaked axe. Inspector Fred Frahm shrugged off the letter as a hoax. "We get many of these notes in murder cases, but nevertheless we have to investigate every clue we get."

One avid newspaper reader disagreed with the chief of detectives' assessment. Examining a reproduction printed in the newspapers, handwriting analyst Agnes V. Hildebrand believed that the killer had indeed penned the note. The proof was evident in the formation of the loops and the heavy lines created when the writer held the pen tightly to the paper. These characteristics, Hildebrandt said, indicated a crude, troglodytic sort of person.

As the investigation neared the end of its first week, Navarre and his team received a fresh set of leads and a new angle to pursue: that somehow, Benny Evangelist had become entangled with the Black Hand, a criminal outfit known for extortion, and may have even acted as the go-between in one of their schemes. Two incidents suggested that organized crime, and not religious mania, motivated the Evangelist killers.

A few years before the massacre, another murder involving Evangelist's nephew Louis Evangelista took place directly across the street from Benny Evangelist's home on St. Aubin Avenue. On February 19, 1926, Louis Evangelista and his father-in-law, Angelo Papraro, ambushed alleged Black Hand lieutenant Felice Argento, supposedly because Argento attempted to extort $5,000 from Papraro. Papraro told police, who planned to show up and nab Argento in the act of collecting the money, but the plan went awry when Argento showed up early. In the ensuing fray, Louis Evangelista shot Argento. Cleared of wrongdoing by a coroner's jury, Evangelista vanished.

A second incident involved building contractor Benny Abruzzi, who told detectives that the Black Hand put the squeeze on him, and Benny Evangelist acted as the middleman. Another piece of the puzzle emerged when a translator finished transcribing the letters found in Evangelist's desk, one of which ended with an ominous threat: "This is your last chance—The Vendetta." Below the pseudonym, the author had drawn the picture of an axe. The axe letter formed the last in a sequence sent by an unidentified extortionist to Evangelist in the year leading up to his murder. The postmark on the "Vendetta" threat indicated that Evangelist received it approximately six months earlier.

These puzzle pieces suggested an entirely different scenario leading up to the Evangelist murders. The Black Hand had extorted Benny Evangelist by demanding protection money. When the healer's resources dwindled to nothing and he could no longer afford to pay, they gave him a choice: squeeze his cult members or go to work for them as a bagman. Hampered by a guilty conscience and seeing no way out, he enlisted the help of neighbors, who killed Felice Argento. The Black Hand retaliated by murdering Evangelist and his entire family. Or, when Benny refused their demands, they sent a strong message to Little Italy by wiping out his family. Or they murdered Evangelist simply because he was the uncle of Argento's shooter.

This scenario explained why Benny Evangelist always appeared strapped for cash despite a thriving industry in cult healing. It also provided a logical backstory for the threatening letter. When Evangelist resisted Black Hand extortion demands or held his ground, they made good on their threat.

Detectives tracked Louis Evangelista to a suburb of Pittsburgh, Pennsylvania, where they found him lying low in an out-of-the-way shack. Visibly agitated, Evangelista said he was the divine prophet's cousin. Fearing for his life, he explained, he fled Detroit after the murder of Argento. Louis Evangelista told everything he knew about the Black Hand and the murder of Argento, but he knew nothing about his uncle's murder. The Argento slaying turned into another dead end. The hot Black Hand lead also fizzled. Tight-lipped denizens of Little Italy, perhaps fearful for their own safety, simply did not want to talk about extortion and extortionists in their neighborhood.

By August 1929, investigators had exhausted all leads. The failure to find a result in the headline case led to a great deal of finger pointing among detectives and the watchdog press. Because so many investigators had jammed into the small Evangelist home, reporters criticized them for conducting a sloppy investigation and destroying vital evidence in the process.

The one usable piece of evidence recovered from the crime scene—the bloody fingerprints found on the door latch—became a source of controversy in the case and scandalized the police department in 1935. For years, police insisted that they had lifted a clear print from the door handle, but according to others, the print had become smudged. Detractors claimed that hasty detectives smudged the print; defenders said that the killer left it that way.

In 1930, Benny the Evangelist rose from the grave when detectives exhumed his body from the Mt. Olivet Cemetery. The cause of this postmortem appearance was a belated attempt to lift a set of fingerprints for comparison with those discovered at a similar crime scene that had occurred ten years earlier in Pennsylvania.

The case that got Evangelist up occurred in 1919 and bore a striking resemblance to what had become known as the Detroit cult murders. The perpetrator, Aurelius Angelino, was a onetime associate of Evangelist. The two men knew each other when Evangelist lived in York, Pennsylvania. They were neighbors and worked together as section hands. Further, they came from the same town in Italy and both were described as "religious fanatics."

In 1919, Aurelius Angelino hacked two of his four children to death with an axe. Angelino escaped three times from asylums, the last time in 1923, when he disappeared. He was also left-handed.

Detectives wondered if some as-yet-unseen thread connected the Angelino and Evangelist cases, which triggered a manhunt for the escaped psychiatric patient. Despite authorities pulling up rocks all over the Midwest, however, Angelino remained underground. The Angelino-Evangelist connection, if any existed, became just another part of the unsolved file. Nevertheless, reporters reveled in this new, macabre angle of the story. "Evangelist's finger pointed from the grave," wrote a *Detroit Times* reporter, "to his former chum, an escaped inmate of a Pennsylvania institution."

With all leads exhausted, the case went cold. Detroit's homicide squad moved on to other cases, but a few doggedly persistent cops continued to chase down leads wherever and whenever they appeared. Most of the time, such leads came from neighborhood gossip—someone heard someone say he saw something—and they went nowhere. In 1935, two new leads resuscitated the once-dead case. For many downtown, this new information closed the file on the Evangelist murders.

The first lead came from an unexpected eyewitness. During the initial investigation, the lack of an eyewitness baffled detectives who were convinced that someone must have seen something. A man wearing blood-drenched clothes could not completely escape notice, even if the crime occurred in the small hours of the morning.

Someone, it turned out, had seen something. Frank Costanza, a fourteen-year-old paperboy in 1929, happened to pass by the Evangelist house at 5:00 a.m. on the morning of July 3. He noticed a familiar figure standing on the porch: Umberto Tecchio, whom detectives pulled in for questioning five hours after the discovery of the bodies. He greeted Tecchio and then continued on his way. When he heard of the killings a few hours later, he became frightened and decided to keep his mouth shut.

Umberto Tecchio died of natural causes on Thanksgiving Day in 1934, so tight lips of once reticent witnesses began to loosen, and Tecchio's once rock-solid alibi began to show stress fractures. Camillo Tress, who occupied a room separated by a thin curtain from the one occupied by Depoli and Tecchio, said he awoke at 6:00 a.m. on July 3 and noticed that Tecchio was not in his bed. Detectives also heard an unsubstantiated story that when Tecchio returned to the boardinghouse that morning, he carried a bag about three feet long—about the size needed to conceal a hatchet or banana knife. Tecchio's roommate at the boardinghouse, Angelo Depoli, may have proved vital at this point in the probe, but after the 1929 investigation, immigration authorities deported him to Italy.

The second lead came from Tecchio's ex-wife, who told detectives that Benny Evangelist's office once contained two machetes. She saw them hanging on the wall when her husband took her to see Benny the healer. During the 1929 sweep of the crime scene, no long knives were found—it now appeared that Tecchio had transported them in a bag, which may have also contained his blood-saturated clothes. No one at the boardinghouse, however, could verify the existence of the bag, perhaps because it ended up at the bottom of the Detroit River about two miles distant from the crime scene.

Umberto Tecchio's quick temper and sudden, unpredictable and violent outbursts made him an ideal suspect. In April 1929, he shot and killed his wife's brother, which ended their marriage. His ex-wife received the house in their divorce settlement. When she remarried and the newlyweds settled into the house, Tecchio, convinced she had defrauded him out of the property, threatened to blow up the house and everyone inside. Her new husband, Louis Peruzzi, went to the police, but they dismissed Tecchio's threat as nothing more than the rantings of a jealous ex-husband. Shortly after reporting the threat, in 1932, Louis Peruzzi supposedly shot himself on his front porch.

Tecchio's death prevented the closure that would result from a trial, but some detectives nonetheless felt that they could finally close the book on the St. Aubin Avenue massacre. A match between his fingerprints and those taken from the latch of Benny Evangelist's front door would prove it.

This led to a fierce debate about the viability of the fingerprints lifted from the scene. During the investigation, Navarre's men wrenched the door latch off the frame and took it to police headquarters, where Inspector Charles Carmody of the fingerprint bureau lauded the prints as flawless. For years, top brass of the Detroit PD stood by the prints as viable evidence. To those on the inside, however, the "flawless" prints became an inside joke. Water cooler wags joked that detectives need look no further than the flatfoots who worked the crime scene for a match; some careless cop had either left the key piece of evidence himself or destroyed its evidentiary value by smudging it.

The reemergence of Umberto Tecchio as a prime albeit dead suspect created a sticky situation for Carmody and the Detroit police because the fingerprints, once heralded as perfect examples, became the focal point of the investigation. Supposedly, detectives checked Tecchio's fingerprints against the latch prints when they hauled him in for questioning in 1929.

Now, after studying Tecchio's fingerprint card, Carmody declared that he could positively identify two similarities between the fingerprints and those of Umberto Tecchio. Chief of Detectives Fred Frahm, who had to swallow unrelenting criticism about the soundness of the 1929 investigation, hit the ceiling when he heard of Carmody's conclusion. He called the fingerprint guru into his office and demanded an explanation. Carmody, he pointed out, did not declare such similarities six years earlier.

"Oh yes I did," Carmody shot back. The two nearly came to blows before cooler heads prevailed. Frahm called for John Navarre, who said that Carmody did not mention any possible match during the original investigation. Frahm asked Lieutenant Charles Donaldson, of the Identification Bureau, to settle the dispute. After studying the two sets of prints, he did not think there was a clear enough match to stand up in court.

Upon hearing Donaldson's conclusion, Frahm declared, "Well, since you can't agree, we will get an expert opinion on the matter. I don't want to close the case until we are sure. Tecchio is dead and can't answer the charges now." The sets of prints went to the Justice Department as well as the Chicago, New York and St. Louis Police Departments. The consensus opinion was that the prints did not match.

Despite the controversy, the department viewed the fingerprints as credible or at least presented them as credible to the press. As late as 1943, the *Detroit Free Press* reported that in the fifteen-year period following the murders, detectives compared these fingerprints with those found at every crime scene involving an axe murder in the United States. Umberto Tecchio's involvement with the crime, if any, remains speculative.

Three distinct theories emerged during the investigation.

1. UMBERTO TECCHIO MURDERED THE EVANGELIST FAMILY OVER A DISPUTE INVOLVING A REAL ESTATE DEBT.

The paperboy's eyewitness account places him on Evangelist's front porch at about the time the killer would have left the premises, and his alibi for the time frame of the murders is shaky at best. Two factors tend to discount Tecchio as a suspect: the lack of bloody clothing and his pattern of violent behavior.

The murders, which were committed with a heavy- or broad-bladed weapon, would have left the perpetrator dripping with blood, yet not one scrap of bloodstained clothing was found at the crime scene. Costanza's statement indicates that he must have been close enough to recognize Tecchio in the faint light of dawn, but he said nothing of Tecchio's clothes, an odd omission if Tecchio left the house covered in Evangelist blood.

Writing about the case in 1948, *Detroit Free Press* crime reporter Royce Howes suggested that the perpetrator might have carried a change of clothes. This scenario places a sinister significance on the bag that Tecchio allegedly carried into the boardinghouse, a bag that potentially concealed two machetes, a pair of shoes and a suit of clothes.

Howes contemplated a second possibility: the slayer committed the murders in the buff, which would explain the lack of bloodstained clothes at the scene. However, as Howes pointed out, there was no evidence that the killer washed up before leaving the residence.

Ironically, the lack of bloodstained clothing at the scene tended to discount Tecchio as a suspect. If the Evangelist killer brought a spare set of clothes, or committed the crime in the nude, he must have carefully planned it. Yet Umberto Tecchio's violent history involved rage crimes and not cold, calculated, premeditated murder.

Besides, a revenge killing to right some perceived wrong over a real estate transaction does not fit with the cult elements evidently taken from or inspired by Evangelist's bible (unless the killer wanted to obscure his true motive): the removal of Benny Evangelist's head and the attempt to sever the victims' arms. It also does not explain the deaths of Santina Evangelist and the four children.

2. A BLACK HAND OPERATIVE MURDERED THE EVANGELIST FAMILY.

Benny Evangelist made a good living in his dual pursuits of real estate and faith healing, except he always seemed to be short of money. Friends also said that in the days leading up to the murders, he appeared nervous, even shaken by something.

Perhaps the strongest piece of evidence supporting the Black Hand theory comes from the sheaf of letters found in Evangelist's bureau, one of which contained a clear threat with a not-so-subtle hand-drawn axe below the signature "Vendetta." Yet the timing of the "Vendetta" letter is problematic. Postmarked six months before the murders, the "last-chance" missive leaves an implausible six-month gap before the Black Hand made good on its threat.

On the other hand, the Black Hand theory provides a plausible explanation for the murder of the entire family. The bloody footprints at the scene of the crime indicated that the killer first dispatched Evangelist and then crept up the stairs and into the first bedroom, where he attacked Evangelist's wife. The placement of the bodies and angles of the wounds indicated that Santina Evangelist was either asleep at the time or had just awoken. The killer clearly did not murder the Evangelist family to prevent them from identifying him later, so why did they have to die?

Extortionists ruled Little Italy through fear, and perhaps they wanted to send a message to the community about the futility of resistance. Father Beccherini, who received multiple Black Hand letters threatening his life, did not believe that extortionists were behind the Evangelist slayings and proposed an alternate supposition. In an interview with the *Detroit Times*, he expressed his "evil eye" theory.

"It is my belief that the murder was committed by someone who was convinced Evangelist had put the 'Mallochio'—the evil eye, on him, or on some member of his family," Beccherini explained. "It was not a blackhand murder, as blackhanders do not work that way—they do not kill the entire family. The evil eye superstition still exists in our Italian colony. Many times I have had people tell me that they would shoot on sight any one who they were convinced had cast the 'Mallochio' upon them." People in Evangelist's neighborhood believed that he had the power to cast the "evil eye."

3. A MEMBER OF EVANGELIST'S CULT COMMITTED THE MURDERS.

The crime scene contained unmistakable references to Benny Evangelist's *Oldest History of the World*; the placement of his head at the feet of his decapitated corpse and the slashes over the shoulders on some of the victims indicated a familiarity with Evangelist's cult teachings.

The timing of the murder, when Evangelist communed with the clouds, also suggests a knowledge of his nightly regimen. Only someone in Evangelist's inner circle would know that between the hours of midnight and 3:00 a.m. he entered a trancelike-fugue state and would not hear footsteps behind him.

The religious mania theory, in which someone murdered the cult's divine prophet out of some slight real or imagined, was a popular one in the early days of the investigation. Maybe the penultimate clue remains buried somewhere in Evangelist's three-hundred-page bible.

The Evangelist case remains on ice. Perhaps a new clue, such as the chance discovery of a bag containing two machetes and a set of blood-drenched clothes half buried in the bottom sediment of the Detroit River, will one day come to the surface and bring closure to one of Michigan's most baffling crimes.

5

He Talked Too Much

Jerry Buckley
(Detroit, 1930)

There was no shortage of suspects in the 1930 slaying of a Detroit radio personality. For police, Gerald E. "Jerry" Buckley represented the worst type of victim: a man with dozens of enemies, most from the Detroit underworld. A fiery anti-crime crusader who used a microphone at WMBC radio station to raise the heat on gangland figures, Buckley's on-air sermons reached thousands and made him a household name. They also made him a target.

A native Detroiter, Buckley spent his youth in old Corktown. The son of affluent landowner J.C. Buckley, he matured into a handsome young man and quickly earned a reputation as a playboy. With an ear for music, he occasionally wrote his own compositions—a talent that made him popular among eligible ladies.

He briefly worked as an investigator for the Ford Motor Company and later used his sleuthing skills doing private jobs for his brother George, a lawyer. With a voice for radio, he eventually became a host for WMBC. By this time, Prohibition had turned Buckley's beloved hometown into a modern-day Gomorrah, which deeply disturbed the popular radio personality. When not calling out corrupt officials and crime lords, Buckley lobbied for social causes, such as rising unemployment and pensions. His civic activism earned him the nickname "voice of the people."

The fiery broadcaster, radio personality and "voice of the people" Gerald E. "Jerry" Buckley. *Walter P. Reuther Library, Archives of Labor and Urban Affairs, Wayne State University.*

By the summer of 1930, Jerry Buckley's two-year-old career on the airwaves had reached its apex, but his personal life had begun to unravel. His eighteen-year marriage to Jeannette was on the rocks, possibly because of a fling with vaudeville actress Jean Alexander, with whom he had exchanged a torrid series of love letters and amorous telegrams. Buckley also began spending more and more time with Evelyn O'Hara, billed as his "personal secretary." The twenty-something secretary was nearly young enough to be the thirty-nine-year-old's daughter, and interestingly, she worked for Buckley without pay.

A newspaper correspondent, writing of Buckley's "assassination" in the July 23, 1930 edition of the *Detroit Times*, hinted at an affair when he described Buckley's separation from Jeannette and then, in the next sentence, wrote, "Several weeks Buckley has been in constant company with Evelyn O'Hara, his personal secretary." Curiously, Buckley never told O'Hara about his wife. O'Hara did not learn about her boss's marital status until after his murder.

Jerry Buckley's pulpit consisted of a radio studio located on the mezzanine of the LaSalle Hotel from which he waged a personal crusade against the city's purveyors of vice. Prohibition-era Detroit had vices aplenty, including a booming trade in illicit liquor, narcotics and prostitution. Police officers and county officials took payoffs to look the other way. A good example of

Detroit officialdom's laxity in controlling consumption of alcohol is the fact that reporters routinely acquired five-gallon tubs of confiscated booze from the city jail.

Sin was big business, and gangs waged war to control the various rackets. Gangland violence turned Detroit into the Wild West, where feuding outfits traded lead in the streets. By the end of the decade, the violence had gotten out of hand. No fewer than eleven gangland slayings occurred in the first three weeks of July 1930, which earned the sobriquet "bloody July."

The violence hit close to home for Buckley when a gangland slaying occurred on the street outside the LaSalle Hotel, located at the corner of Woodward Avenue and Adelaide Street. On July 3, two Chicago-based racketeers—William Cannon and George Collins—went down in a hailstorm of bullets just minutes before Buckley went on the air. Infuriated with the latest example of the city's unchecked violence, Buckley issued an ultimatum to authorities: find the killers or he would identify them in a future broadcast.

Buckley must have spent a fair amount of time talking to informants who moved among the criminal underworld. "He delivered a wealth of detailed information about handbooks, blind pigs, houses of ill repute and other subjects," recalled *Free Press* reporter Riley Murray, who often obtained fodder from the radio personality. "And it checked out accurately."

The newly elected Mayor Charles Bowles provided the radio jockey with plenty of fodder.

The summer of 1930 was a busy time for Jerry Buckley. Mayor Bowles was at the center of a vicious recall campaign that had begun the previous May and stemmed from an incident involving underground drinking establishments. Disgusted with the runaway vice problems in Detroit, reporters hounded Harold Emmons, the police commissioner, to conduct a series of raids on blind pigs and gambling dens. Emmons obliged, and Bowles promptly fired him, which raised the specter of graft in city hall and triggered a recall campaign.

The embattled mayor's administration became the subject of Jerry Buckley's angst with the city's runaway violence and the target of his on-air invective. During one broadcast, Buckley likened Bowles to Emperor Nero by suggesting that the mayor fiddled while Rome burned. The comparison was clear: crime flourished under Bowles's administration even though the mayor had promised to clean up Sin City of the Midwest.

Despite his bitter enmity toward Bowles, Buckley actually opposed the recall, instead favoring an impeachment, which would cost the taxpayers less.

The opulent LaSalle Hotel, rechristened the Detroiter Hotel in 1931. *Walter P. Reuther Library, Archives of Labor and Urban Affairs, Wayne State University.*

John Gillespie, the commissioner of public works and a close associate of Bowles, later said that Buckley went to him on July 18 with a speech opposing the mayor's recall. Then he made an astonishing about-face and planned to go on the air that night to read a speech promoting the recall effort.

Ten minutes before Buckley was to give the speech, his station manager received a threatening phone call. If Buckley went on the air in promotion of the recall effort, the unidentified caller said, he would be "taken for a long ride." Buckley ignored the warning and charred the mayor on his nightly broadcast, which took place an hour later than usual. For the first time, Buckley openly accused Bowles of being in bed with known underworld figures.

On Thursday, July 22, 1930, Bowles was on the verge of losing his job, in part due to Buckley's relentless smear campaign and caustic editorializing. And by late July 1930, Jerry Buckley was "on the spot."

Like Julius Caesar's Ides of March, there were omens that foreshadowed the fateful moment in the lobby of the LaSalle Hotel. *Detroit Free Press* reporter Riley Murray, who periodically obtained inside information from Buckley, spoke to his deep throat a few days before the murder and warned about possible reprisals. Murray had heard that Buckley "was on the spot."

Murray suggested a precaution: Buckley should jot out a list of those who most likely wanted to harm him, place the list in a safety deposit box and then tell everyone who would listen about it. The second key to the bank box, Buckley should say, was in the hands of a secret source. The list of "usual suspects," coupled with the nameless source (Murray) who could take the list to police at any minute, would act as a deterrent to any would-be assassins.

Writing about the crime twenty-five years later, Murray recalled Buckley's reaction. "After pondering the idea for a while," Murray said in a 1955 article about the case, "his face lighted in a smile. Then he said: 'I'll be all right.'" Famous last words.

Buckley may have felt insulated by his position as a radio personality, perhaps buoyed by the belief that a public figure remained out-of-bounds for mob hit men. He carried a gun just in case.

Several Buckley anecdotes that emerged in the succeeding months, some of them possibly apocryphal, illustrated the Teflon image he projected in public. He received dozens of threatening letters and phone calls, none of which daunted him. Death threats, which Buckley once joked came in at twenty a day, were the proof that his radio broadcasts had hit mobsters where it hurt, in the family jewels. He remained steadfast when confronted by no fewer than eleven gangsters who warned him to keep his mouth shut or else.

Buckley's jocularity about being "taken for a ride" may have been bravado. Friends of the thirty-nine-year-old said that he sometimes remained holed up in his LaSalle room for several days at a time. "He recently had developed a marked apprehension because of the threatening letters he had received," Evelyn O'Hara later recalled. Like Riley Murray, O'Hara urged Buckley to watch his back, but he just shrugged off her concerns. With typical bravado, he remarked, "When the time comes I'll be killed, and there's no use trying to stave it off."

Buckley spent Tuesday night, July 22, 1930, at city hall broadcasting the recall election returns from a microphone specially set up by the station. The successful recall represented triumph for Bowles detractors, a triumph over organized crime and a step closer to curtailing vice rackets in Detroit.

In his broadcast, Buckley offered a few words of comfort to his listeners. "We will all be here after it [the recall] is over with, and we will all be ready to take part in the next political campaign," he said, "and maybe next time we'll all be on the same side. Who can tell?"

After the broadcast, he returned to the LaSalle with Evelyn O'Hara. O'Hara noticed fear bordering on paranoia in her boss, who apparently worried about being taken for a ride. "When we took a taxi to the hotel," she said, "he looked carefully at the driver before getting in. When he got out at the hotel he looked both ways first and then paid the driver and hurriedly entered the hotel."

According to bellhop William Adams, at about 12:15 a.m., Buckley walked O'Hara through the lobby, helped her into a taxi, then turned and went back into the hotel lobby, where he asked for his mail. Buckley asked Adams "where the party was," made a call from the house phone and then went to a party hosted by a friend on the eleventh floor.

Sometime around 12:45 a.m. on the morning of Wednesday, July 23, 1930, Buckley received a phone call from a woman. The owner of WMBC, who overheard Buckley's side of the conversation, indicated that Buckley apparently thought he was talking to his sister Mary. After Buckley said, "In about an hour," he hung up the receiver. Other sources have Buckley saying, "It's a date. I'll see you in the lobby."

About forty-five minutes later, he briefly paused to pick up a copy of the *Detroit Free Press*, mused at the front-page story, "SINISTER INFLUENCES CONTROL MAYOR," and continued to scan the headlines as he plopped down in a large chair.

Meanwhile, a black sedan slowed to a stop in front of the Adelaide Street entrance to the LaSalle. According to Gus Reno, a cab driver parked in front of the hotel, two men stepped out of the vehicle and joined a third at the hotel entrance. The three men then went into the building.

At approximately 1:45 a.m. (contemporary news accounts place the time at 1:44 a.m.), three figures appeared in front of Buckley as he sat reading the news. He stood from the chair, but before he could utter a word, two of them leveled their revolvers at him and emptied the guns, each firing six shots. Of the dozen bullets, eleven struck Buckley, who fell face-first to the floor.

Above: The Buckley crime scene inside the LaSalle Hotel. Buckley was sitting in one of the two chairs and reading the newspaper when his slayers approached him. *Walter P. Reuther Library, Archives of Labor and Urban Affairs, Wayne State University.*

Opposite: Another view of the Buckley crime scene. Newspapers covered the bloodstained carpet, marking the spot where Buckley fell. The bullets left two tears in the chair upholstery. *Walter P. Reuther Library, Archives of Labor and Urban Affairs, Wayne State University.*

The two gunmen scurried out of the LaSalle and jumped into the back seat of the sedan, which roared down Woodward. A second car, driven by a woman with another woman in the passenger seat, jackknifed across traffic in what looked like an attempt to block anyone who might attempt a chase.

The police did not broadcast an all-points bulletin over the radio, Thomas Wilcox later explained, because they had no eyewitnesses who could describe the killers. Later, it became public that the police did have eyewitnesses but did not use the police radio, which some critics said amounted to helping the killers flee and represented either gross negligence, or worse, a high-level conspiracy to cover up their identities.

The assassination sent shock waves throughout Michigan. Detroiters lost the dauntless crusader who dared venture where they would not, and local authorities faced enormous pressure to solve Buckley's murder. Governor Fred Green visited Detroit and detailed a special state police squad to join the hunt. Police commissioner and former FBI agent Thomas Wilcox took charge of the investigation and put every available man on the hunt for clues around the clock. He also tapped Fred Frahm, head of the Homicide Squad, as his field general.

As a testament to the radio announcer's immense popularity, thousands of people queued up for a chance to shuffle past his body as he lay in state at his Pasadena Avenue home. An estimated seventy-five thousand spectators lined the streets as the funeral procession crawled toward Mt. Olivet Cemetery on Saturday, July 26, 1930.

"Who killed Jerry Buckley" became a rallying cry throughout the city. The chants also became a notice to police that Detroiters wanted justice in the slaying of the man known as the "voice of the people."

Curious onlookers line the streets during the funeral procession of Jerry Buckley. *Author's collection.*

In the days and weeks following that fatal day in the LaSalle lobby, Buckley's murder—and the sinister forces behind it—became the topic of conversation across the city. Everyone had a pet theory, but during the investigation, four distinct scenarios emerged.

Because Buckley apparently reveled in haranguing vice lords during his broadcasts and habitually named names, the first theory also presented the most problems for investigators: someone iced Buckley to settle a score, act on a vendetta or protect a racket. The list of usual suspects in this scenario ran into the dozens.

Another line of inquiry revolved around the recall of Mayor Bowles and his underworld supporters. Buckley made no bones about his distaste for Bowles and hammered away at the mayor with a relentless barrage of on-air criticism. Sources credit Buckley's broadcasts for the successful recall, which would have incensed gangsters who subsequently lost their major connection downtown. Jerry's brother Paul, a former assistant prosecuting attorney, favored this line. "Jerry died because of the part he took in campaigning for the recall of Mayor Charles Bowles," he said the day after his brother's assassination.

Buckley did not receive one red cent from WMBC, according to studio manager W. Wright Gedge. Instead, he earned his money—an estimated $1,000 in the two years as "voice of the people"—from commissions, which included money from competing interests in the recall of Mayor Bowles. This put a sinister slant on the supposed conversation he had had with Bowles's confederate John Gillespie on the eve of the recall election and just before the radio broadcast in which he first promoted the recall effort. According to Gillespie, Buckley offered to sell him a "silent interest" in WMBC for $30,000, which Gillespie understood to represent control of "the political policy of the station through Buckley."

"I told him $30,000 was a lot of money," Gillespie later recalled. "He said if I would pay $15,000 down and the rest in a week it would be all right."

According to Gillespie, Buckley sounded desperate. "He said: 'I've really got to have $15,000 right away. Will you advance me that on the prospect of going through with the sale after the election?'" Gillespie did not ante up $15,000, and although he did not allege that Buckley tried to squeeze him for payment, the bottom line was that suddenly and unexpectedly, Buckley reversed his position on the mayor's recall.

Two obvious problems undermined the theory that Buckley's position on the recall cost him his life. Clifford Prevost, a writer for the *Detroit Free Press*, made Bowles a target of numerous scathing articles and undoubtedly played a role in the mayor's downfall. Yet Prevost never became an assassin's target.

Besides, the timing of Buckley's murder made little sense if major underworld figures wanted to keep Buckley from helping overthrow Bowles. The shooting took place after the recall election, after it became clear that the voters had already run Bowles out of office.

Another theory tied Buckley's murder to the gangland slaying of Cannon and Collins, the racketeers gunned down outside of the LaSalle Hotel on July 3, 1930. While most sources agreed that Buckley could not have seen the incident from his studio, the *Detroit Times* reported that they received information from "authentic sources" that Buckley was gazing out of a window when he happened to see the shootings. According to the omnipresent Evelyn O'Hara, who was with Buckley in the locked recording studio that day, he first heard of the shooting when someone slipped a note underneath the door. Regardless, he more than hinted that he could finger the triggermen when he threatened to identity them in a future broadcast. They may have iced him before he had the chance.

Detectives also followed a line that possibly connected Buckley to shady business dealings, including blackmail and kidnapping. One allegation had Buckley using his radio show as a bully pulpit to extort hush money from underworld figures. If they failed to pay for his silence, he threatened to out them on the air. Gillespie alluded to such blackmail when he hinted that Buckley offered to dial down his criticism in exchange for a fee, which if true would explain how he transformed from a recall opponent into a proponent on July 18.

A known kidnapper named Stanley DeLong said that Buckley acted as the "fingerman" in a kidnapping ring, or the member of the cabal who identified potential victims with relatives wealthy enough to pay ransoms. Although DeLong later repudiated his statements, the dead man received a roasting at the typewriters of newspapermen in the days following his execution.

According to another rumor, Buckley had somehow become entangled in a gangland feud. Two major players in the illicit trade of alcohol were kidnapped in their hometown of Windsor and held for ransom. Their associates retaliated by ensuring the arrest of Frank Cammarata and Yonny Licovoli, two powerful crime figures in Detroit, on illegal weapons charges. As the story went, Buckley acted as the middleman or bagman to handle a sizable cash payment to release the gangsters, then reneged on the deal.

Because detectives explored these possibilities, Jerry's brother Paul, a former assistant prosecutor, accused Wilcox of tarring his brother's name. These unfounded allegations, he believed, amounted to nothing less than a character assassination, meaning that Jerry Buckley had been murdered a second time during the Wilcox-Frahm investigation.

Police identified the woman driving the car that screeched across Woodward Avenue in an apparent attempt at creating a roadblock as Lucille Love, the daughter of a cop and a resident of the LaSalle. Love provided an innocent explanation. Upon hearing the gunshots emanating from the hotel lobby, she slammed on the brakes. Terrified, she and her friend ran off, abandoning the automobile in the center of the street.

They had no such luck finding the woman who made the call that allegedly set up Buckley.

The telephone call from "Mary," which at first appeared an innocuous, mundane detail, now assumed sinister overtones. Buckley may have mistaken the caller's voice for his sister's, but more than likely, "Mary" impersonated Buckley's sister. Either way, the phone call indicated that the perpetrators carefully orchestrated the murder.

Over the next several days, a parade of dubious women walked into and out of the investigation. Police netted cabaret dancers, molls, prostitutes and bottle smugglers in their attempt to identify the woman who put Buckley on the spot by luring him to the lobby of the LaSalle.

A prime candidate for the voice was vaudeville actress Jean Alexander. Baskets of letters told of an affaire de coeur between Buckley and Alexander, a tryst that apparently soured. According to Evelyn O'Hara, Buckley feared the woman scorned and once remarked that he felt threatened by her. Alexander could have made the call; she was in Detroit, performing at the Fox Theater. Despite a relentless grilling, however, detectives could not pair Alexander with the fateful and fatal phone call.

Detectives received a hot tip when cab driver Gus Reno told of seeing Angelo Livecchi, a known hood, loitering around the LaSalle at around the time of the Buckley shooting. According to the cabbie, who was parked outside the hotel, Livecchi went in and out of the Adelaide Street entrance no fewer than eight times in the minutes before Buckley was shot. When the sedan pulled to the curb, Livecchi followed the two men into the lobby.

Livecchi lived at the LaSalle, which made his presence at the hotel less than sinister, but his shady background nevertheless made him a prime suspect. Frahm's boys collared him in his room and subjected him to days of relentless grilling. Wilcox, convinced of Livecchi's involvement, proclaimed him "the lookout man for the killers." Frahm's team also wanted to talk to "Black Leo" Cellura, whom Evelyn O'Hara saw bully Buckley around a week before the murder, but he was nowhere to be found.

Following Angelo Livecchi's footprints through the maze of underworld Detroit, investigators would eventually identify the men they believed responsible for Buckley's hit.

The intense pressure on authorities to bring Buckley's killers to justice resulted in a twenty-three-person grand jury, which brought the Sword of Damocles down on the necks of gangsters and corrupt officials alike. Although motivated by the Buckley assassination, the grand jury looked into hundreds of unsolved crimes and allegations of corruption from local police precincts to city hall. Over its lifespan, it handed down over fifty indictments, including eight for the LaSalle lobby slaying: Angelo Livecchi, "Scarface" Joe Bommarito, Theodore Pizzino, Peter Licavoli and three unidentified accomplices dubbed "John Doe," "Richard Roe" and "Mary Roe," the woman who made the call that apparently led Jerry Buckley to his death.

Angelo Livecchi was the first domino to fall. His presence at the LaSalle at the time of the murder caused three additional dominoes to fall; his association with known underworld figures Theodore Pizzino (his roommate at the LaSalle), "Scarface" Joe Bommarito and crime boss Peter Licavoli led to their subsequent indictments. Licavoli's girlfriend was a prime candidate for the voiceover of "Mary," although the possibility remained speculative; no one other than the deceased had heard her voice. "Black" Leo Cellura, who remained on the lam, dodged an indictment.

In 1931, Livecchi, Bommarito and Pizzino faced the music together in court. Peter Licavoli stood alone in a separate trial.

The trial occurred in a circus-like atmosphere peopled by journalists and the typical court-goers, all of whom crammed into the courtroom to witness what they believed might be the last act in the sordid tragedy of Jerry Buckley's murder. It was a trial characterized by allegations of perjury and purchased testimony. The hoods on trial were known bad men, but some believed that the state manufactured witnesses to secure convictions in a case that prosecutors could not afford to lose.

The prosecution, led by Harry S. Toy, relied on a paper-thin motive for the crime. "We claim Buckley was attacking the racketeers and that's why he was killed," Toy said in describing the gist of his case.

The case against Livecchi hinged on three eyewitnesses who saw him at the LaSalle when the murder occurred. Taxi driver Gus Reno testified about watching, from the vantage point of his cab parked on Woodward Avenue, the defendant drift into and out of the hotel eight separate times. On one trip, Livecchi appeared to lead two men from the black sedan into the hotel lobby. Scurrying into the hotel, the trio nearly ran over Fred Tara, a sometime police informant who just happened to be standing outside of the Adelaide Street entrance. LaSalle night porter Robert Jackson testified to seeing Livecchi standing behind the two shooters when they unloaded their revolvers into Buckley.

Angelo Livecchi in court during the Buckley trial in March 1931. *Walter P. Reuther Library, Archives of Labor and Urban Affairs, Wayne State University.*

The case against Theodore Pizzino appeared equally damning. He shared a room at the LaSalle with Angelo Livecchi and left Detroit a few days after the murder. Investigators ran him down in New York just as he was about to close an account containing money recently wired from Detroit. Packed suitcases indicated that Pizzino planned to skip town. Robert Davidson, who was at city hall when the recall election returns came in, overheard a man he later identified as Pizzino say, "If Bowles loses this recall, don't forget what we've got to do tonight." Fred Tara fingered Pizzino as one of the men who almost knocked him over, and Robert Jackson identified Pizzino as one of the men he saw from the dining room window climbing into the black sedan after the shooting.

The case against "Scarface" Joe Bommarito hinged on the testimony of Robert Jackson, who named him as the other man he saw jump into the

Above: Ted Pizzino stares at the photographer while his lawyer, Allen Kent, examines the indictment. *Walter P. Reuther Library, Archives of Labor and Urban Affairs, Wayne State University.*

Left: Ted Pizzino behind bars. *Walter P. Reuther Library, Archives of Labor and Urban Affairs, Wayne State University.*

black sedan. Neither Tara nor Reno could identify "Scarface" as one of the men they saw outside of the hotel.

Fred Tara marred his own credibility and severely damaged the prosecution's case when, in mid-trial, he stopped talking during the defense cross-examination. Terrified of recriminations, he refused to let press photographers snap his picture. When one of them managed to get a shot, Tara refused to testify, which earned him a stint behind bars for contempt of court. He even went on a hunger strike. Eventually, Fred Tara returned to the witness box, but his on-again, off-again cooperation tainted his testimony.

The defense peppered the prosecution's case by pointing out contradictions in the testimony of the state's star witnesses. The accounts of Reno and Tara differed in the details, such as the clothing worn by the men they saw enter the LaSalle. Defense attorneys, in asking each witness about the twenty-five-dollar-a-week allowance, further undermined the state's case by hinting that the prosecution purchased testimony.

Most damaging to the prosecution's case was the testimony of several witnesses who provided sharply contrasting accounts. A car salesman in the LaSalle lobby at the time of the shooting was close enough to see the shooters' faces. "It was such an expression," he recalled on the stand, "that if you saw it once you would remember it next time." The faces burned into his memory, he testified, did not belong to any of the defendants.

An electrician named Earl Parker testified to seeing four men rush into the hotel and then, after hearing several gunshots, watching them run out again. He countered the testimony of Gus Reno when he said that the defendants were not the men he saw. Hotel bellhop William Adams, who knew Livecchi and Pizzino as residents of the LaSalle, also testified to seeing the three men gun down Buckley but could not identify the shooters. When asked, "Have you seen the men since the shooting?" by one of the defense attorneys, Adams replied, "No, sir."

Adams said that not once did he ever see Bommarito at the LaSalle and gave a statement to police a few hours after the murder. Despite his vantage point, Adams said, police did not ask him to look at suspects until November, four months later.

W.S. Martin, a sound engineer at WMBC, was sitting by the window of a room on the tenth floor of the LaSalle when he heard gunfire. From his perch at the windowsill, he watched the shooters flee the hotel. Martin said he knew both Livecchi and Pizzino well and testified that none of the men he saw darting out of the LaSalle was either defendant. Martin answered the obvious objection—how could he see so clearly from such a height—

when he explained that one of the men looked upward and the canopy lights illuminated his face.

Evelyn O'Hara took center stage in the fifth week of the trial. *Detroit Times* police reporter Lee J. Smits, well known for a regular column "Sidewalks of Detroit," described Buckley's secretary with the detail of a novelist. She had "large, luminous eyes; the generously formed, highly expressive mouth which suggests unusual intelligence; long hands that are most of the time completely quiet in her lap. No rings. She smiles easily and well, and her teeth are flawless."

If anyone knew the inside dope on Buckley's business dealings, it was the woman with the "large, luminous eyes." O'Hara knew a great deal about Buckley's doings, including the reason behind some scathing remarks he made about Henry Ford, the reason behind the delay of his broadcast on July 18 and the animosity between him and his brother Paul, who was in one of the establishments raided after Buckley named it in a broadcast. Yet her time on the stand was marred by constant objections that had the effect of silencing a witness who left the box knowing more than she told.

What once appeared a foregone conclusion collapsed under a mountain of conflicting testimony, a fact apparent when the jury returned a verdict of "not guilty." Defense attorney Allen Kent, in his closing summation, argued that the prosecution had offered the defendants as "sacrificial victims" to satiate the public's thirst for vengeance in the Buckley case.

Kent characterized the trial as a sham and an attempt to frame three innocent men. If he had the authority, Kent said, "In 60 days I'll put behind the bars of Jackson prison not only detectives in this case but some of your investigators and one of your assistant prosecutors for what has been done." The real killers, Kent noted, escaped when the police failed to broadcast news of Buckley's murder.

The acquittal deflated the state's case against Peter Licavoli. The charges lingered through lengthy delays but were eventually dropped due to a lack of evidence in 1932.

A few months after beating the Buckley rap, Livecchi and Pizzino returned to court for their involvement in the Cannon-Collins murders. Convicted, they each received life sentences. They left prison on parole in 1950 and were promptly deported to Italy. "Black Leo" Cellura, also indicted in the Cannon-Collins murders, remained underground until 1937. When he finally surfaced, he too went to trial for the murders and received a life sentence.

The mass of conflicting testimony, coupled with allegations of perjury, cast doubt on statements made from the witness box and eroded any evidentiary value of the trial record. Still, a few interesting and unexplained facets of the case emerged.

In his closing statement, Pizzino's attorney Allen Kent—a former assistant prosecutor with 181 murder trials behind him—made much of Buckley's hat, which no one could find after the shooting. Buckley did not wear it into the lobby, and detectives did not find it in room 1142. The hat represented part of Kent's attempts to build an alternate theory, to create reasonable doubt for the jury by indicting the Hamtramck "businessmen" in room 1142.

"I want to ask you this one very important question," Kent said to the jurors. "What became of Gerald Buckley's hat that night? Was that hat left in [room 1142] and was the information suppressed by the police. He didn't have a hat on when he came down in the lobby and went to his death. Don't you see that Buckley was sent to his death in that lobby?"

Kent also highlighted the king's ransom of $15,000 that Buckley told Gillespie he needed. Gillespie's testimony suggested that Buckley appeared desperate, which underscored the idea that Buckley's need for the money somehow related to his demise. "Will you tell me why on the Wednesday

Allen Kent, who died when a pistol that he was using in a reenactment accidentally discharged. *Author's collection.*

preceding Buckley's death," Kent asked, "he visited John Gillespie and said 'I must have $15,000 this week'? I wish you would tell me why he did that."

As for the actual triggermen, Kent undoubtedly had suspects in mind. Although he did not mention them by name, he did mention a place when he argued that in not broadcasting the news of the murder, the police allowed the killers to escape to Cicero, Illinois.

This argument incensed Toy, who shot back with an equally powerful piece of reasoning. If Kent knew the killers escaped to Cicero, that information could only have come from the killers, whom Toy wanted jurors to identify as the three men in the dock. "Mr. Kent says the murderers left in a high-powered car and that as dawn was breaking they were entering the outskirts of Cicero (Illinois). Who told him this if it wasn't the actual killers?"

Allan Kent died a year later in a bizarre accident, when a handgun, which he was using in a demonstration, accidentally discharged.

Speaking about the case fifty years later, *Free Press* journalist Riley Murray regretted that Buckley did not heed his advice to take precautions, to write out a list of the usual suspects who would want him out of the way for good. "I'd wish to hell I'd gotten that piece of paper," Murray said. "That piece of paper," if Buckley had followed Murray's advice, would probably not have listed the names Livecchi, Pizzino or Bommarito. Evelyn O'Hara testified that Buckley once said, "I'm not worried about the Dagoes."

The top name on Buckley's list might have belonged to none other than his onetime flame Jean Alexander, whom O'Hara said Buckley absolutely feared for some reason unknown to her. "He told me he was afraid of her right after she came to Detroit," O'Hara said when cross-examined for the defense, "just about two weeks before he was killed."

Like O'Hara, Alexander became one of the starlets of the trial billed as "Michigan's most famous murder trial." *Detroit Times* reporter Vera Brown described the vaudevillian as a "tall, willowy, striking" brunette. Alexander's correspondence to Buckley, two baskets of letters and telegrams, became the center of a minor mystery. Taken from Buckley's room the day after the shooting, the documents ended up in the possession of then police commissioner Thomas Wilcox but subsequently disappeared when he resigned.

In his stormy summation, Allen Kent characterized the story that a woman lured Buckley to his death as "bunk" but nevertheless indicted Alexander as "Mary Roe."

"I'll say," Kent said, "if a woman is indicted for murder in this case, it must be Jean Alexander, the girl without her love, the girl whom Evelyn O'Hara told you Jerry Buckley said he feared, the girl who says, 'I'll go the weary ways alone.'"

Fellow defense attorney Allen Maiullo also doubted if Buckley received a call from a woman who put him "on the spot." Maiullo offered an alternate theory: the signal to the killers came from the switching on (or off) of a light in room 1142, where Buckley was at a party with several Hamtramck men who had powerful underworld connections—men directly threatened by what Buckley might say on the air, men threatened by growing movement to recall the mayor of Hamtramck. "There was a reason for that party at the hotel that night, just before he [Buckley] was killed," Maiullo said in his closing argument. "They had to sacrifice somebody, and they sacrificed Buckley, and that ended the Hamtramck recall."

If true, then Buckley's about-face on the recall of Mayor Bowles may have led to his death after all, not because of the damage done to Bowles but because of the potential damage done to Bowles's colleague in Hamtramck. This theory would explain why Buckley, an ardent critic of Bowles, died only after changing his stance on the eve of the recall vote and not before, when his verbal missiles helped destroy the mayor's political career.

As late as 1980, the Buckley murder investigation reposed in three files containing typed notes, newspaper clippings and photographs gathering dust in the archives of the Detroit police. Police file 2299, the murder of Gerald E. "Jerry" Buckley, remains unsolved to this day.

6

"A Riddle, Wrapped in a Mystery, inside an Enigma"

(Grand Rapids, 1938)

How could a perpetrator, covered in blood, leave a building unobserved in broad daylight? Police confronted this question on March 4, 1938, on the third floor of a Grand Rapids warehouse. The murder of nineteen-year-old stenographer Mina Dekker presents, to borrow a quote from Winston Churchill, a "riddle, wrapped in a mystery, inside an enigma."

"But," as Churchill noted, "perhaps there is a key."

It was business as usual for the three employees of the Behr-Manning Company, a New York–based wholesaler of abrasives, on Friday, March 4, 1938. The Grand Rapids branch of the company occupied the third floor of the four-story Judd Building, located at 64 Ionia Avenue. Manager Charles Blackford, his son Robert and stenographer Mina Dekker worked from an office on the third floor, which also housed the company's inventory. The Manufacturer's Supply Company—the only other occupants of the Judd Building—maintained offices on the ground floor. The second and fourth floors stood vacant.

The pretty nineteen-year-old stenographer had attended South High School. After graduating with the class of 1936 and briefly attending Haney's Commercial College, she took a job with Behr-Manning but still lived at home with her father, Adrian, a janitor and sexton at the Fifth Reformed

Church; mother, Janet; twenty-three-year-old sister, Marie; and fourteen-year-old brother, Adrian Jr.

Mina sang in the church choir and devoted much of her free time to church endeavors, although according to Marie, her efforts at the church had slackened a bit recently. Her long-term relationship with John Schafer, a student at a local business college, had apparently soured a month earlier when Mina eyed him with another woman.

Mina left Behr-Manning at about 11:30 a.m. for lunch. She returned an hour later and began typing a purchase order that Blackford requested. Ten minutes later—

Pretty typist and murder victim Mina Dekker. *Author's collection.*

at 12:40 p.m.—Charles and Robert Blackford went out for lunch, leaving Dekker alone on the third floor.

A few minutes after the Blackfords left for lunch, Herbert Banning, the seventeen-year-old messenger from Western Union, entered the third-floor office to pick up a telegram. Dekker was typing an order when the boy arrived. Dekker appeared nervy, even "startled," by a sound coming from the stockroom. According to Banning, she glanced into the warehouse several times during the few minutes he spent in the office. Banning left the Judd Building and went straight back to the Western Union office, arriving at 12:49 p.m.

What happened during the forty-two-minute period between 12:48 p.m. and 1:30 p.m. became a "riddle, wrapped in a mystery, inside an enigma." During this crucial interval, Arthur H. Leopold, an employee of the Manufacturer's Supply Company, and his colleague Ray Coby ate lunch from their office, located at the front of the building. Leopold later recalled hearing a door slam. Coby thought he heard the freight elevator at the rear of the building.

At 1:30 p.m., a local shoemaker named Ray Peters came into the building to buy sandpaper. He passed through the front entrance and walked up the stairs to the third-floor office, situated next to the stairwell and separated from the stockroom by a series of glass partitions. Finding nobody in the office, Peters turned to leave when he heard the sounds of heavy breathing coming from the stockroom.

Tiptoeing into the stockroom to investigate the source of the breathing, he discovered the body of a woman, lying on her back, in a pool of blood. He shrieked and darted back to the first floor, where he alerted Arthur H. Leopold. "Call an ambulance," he shrieked. "A girl has been badly hurt up there."

Leopold and Manufacturer's Supply Company truck driver Calvin DeBlaey rode the freight elevator to the third floor while Peters remained in his office. After regaining his composure a few minutes later, Peters returned to the third floor. Meanwhile, eyeing the figure on the floorboards, Leopold raced back down to his office and telephoned for an ambulance.

The bad news traveled fast. When police officers arrived a few minutes later, a small crowd had already gathered on the sidewalk outside the Judd Building.

At first, police did not know if they were looking at the scene of an unfortunate accident or something more sinister. If Mina stood on a chair to reach something and fell, hitting her head on the floor, then an overturned chair or box would have told the tale. Nothing in the storeroom suggested such a scenario. As the extent of Mina Dekker's wounds became evident, it became equally clear that they were looking at a crime scene. Dr. E.M. Roth, the family physician who tended to Mina in the hospital, dismissed the possibility of an accident when he said that the wounds "could not have been inflicted unless she was slammed down."

Over the next two hours, Mina Dekker lingered in a comatose state. While doctors fought to save the nineteen-year-old, a squad of detectives under the direction of Grand Rapids police chief Frank O'Malley, Inspector Albert Scheien and Detectives Frank Breen and Anning Taylor combed the crime scene for clues.

A large pool of blood marked the spot where Mina Dekker lay on the floor, about forty yards into the stockroom from her desk and between stacks of boxes containing sandpaper. Lines of blood spatter covered the boxes as high as three feet from the floor. A fragment of bone, dislodged from the victim's skull, was found on the floorboards.

The typewriter on Mina's desk contained a half-completed work order, which suggested that Mina was typing when she left her desk to go into the stockroom. Her gloves and purse sat on another desk in the office.

A pool of blood marks the spot where an unknown assailant attacked Mina Dekker. *Grand Rapids Police Department.*

Warehouse where the Mina Dekker murder occurred in 1938. *Grand Rapids Police Department.*

Above: Crime scene photograph showing the second-story entrance to the freight elevator at the back of the Judd Building. *Grand Rapids Police Department.*

Left: On the day of Mina Dekker's murder, detectives found these notes on a sheet of lined paper in her purse. *Grand Rapids Police Department.*

The items in Dekker's purse represented a microcosm of the nineteen-year-old's life: a tube of lipstick, a compact and several pieces of personal correspondence including a small sheet of notebook paper containing two handwritten drafts of a note. The first draft read, "May I give you just a few words of advice? Please do not hurt the next girl you love." The second draft read, "May I give you just a few words of advice? Please ~~show~~ be a little more considerate of the next girl you fall in love with." Dekker had crossed out the word *show* and replaced it with *be*, which she had written above the stricken word. She signed the note, "A friend whose feelings have been terribly hurt. Mina" Another note, apparently written to a friend, alluded to a break-up and contained the line, "It seems strange not going out with him, but I'm not going back until I'm good and ready."

Whoever bludgeoned Mina Dekker chose the ideal setting, and the ideal time, to get away with murder. The assailant could have accessed the third floor through the stairwell at the front of the building, a set of emergency stairs at the back of the building or the freight elevator at the back of the building. More than likely, he avoided the front entrance, where he would have passed by Leopold and Coby, who were eating lunch in the M.S.C. office, and instead used the freight elevator.

Once on the third floor, he could do whatever he wanted and no one would hear a sound. Even if Dekker managed to utter a scream, the vacant floor sandwiched between the first and third muffled any sounds emanating from the Behr-Manning storeroom.

Although a contingent of detectives conducted an exhaustive search of the building that lasted throughout the rest of the day, they came up empty-handed. No bloodstained clothes, no droplets of blood in either stairwell or the freight elevator and no murder weapon. The best guess had the blood-drenched perpetrator taking the freight elevator to the ground floor, managing to evade notice and tossing the murder weapon in the Grand River, where swift currents could wash away blood and fingerprints and within hours embed it under a blanket of muddy effluent.

The motive was equally baffling. Behr-Manning did most of its business through wholesale orders, so the office did not contain a large amount of cash and nothing was missing from the stockroom. It was not surprising that the killer managed to sneak into the building unobserved; he could have hidden on of the vacant floors and waited for the opportune moment to strike. Just how he managed to escape notice while walking down the street in blood-drenched clothes, however, mystified detectives.

Chief O'Malley hoped that someone had seen a suspicious character scurrying down the street dripping blood. "It would appear reasonable that whoever struck the blows which caused this death must have gathered some blood on their clothing. Someone may have seen such a person. Maybe the break will come from this direction."

Mina Dekker died at 3:05 p.m. on March 4—ninety-five minutes after she was discovered sprawled out on the floorboards of the Behr-Manning warehouse—at St. Mary's Hospital without regaining consciousness. Her death record lists the cause of death as "fracture of skull."

She sustained five different head wounds inflicted with a blunt object: on the top of her head, at the base of her skull, over her left temple, behind her left ear and behind her right ear. Because these blows led to several skull fractures, Kent County coroner Dr. Simeon Leroy believed that the killer struck her with a heavy object such as a claw hammer. Any one of the five blows would have proved fatal. The other four were overkill.

In addition to abrasions on her face, Mina Dekker sustained a bone fracture in her right pinkie finger, most likely when she raised her arm in an attempt to shield herself from one of the blows. She did not appear to have been sexually assaulted.

Mina Dekker's wounds and the evidence uncovered at the crime scene suggested a likely scenario for the attack. The perpetrator waited for Charles and Robert Blackford to go to lunch, which left Mina Dekker alone. The assailant rode the freight elevator to the third-floor stockroom, but the arrival of the Western Union boy interrupted his plan. He waited for the boy to leave and accidentally bumped into something, causing a noise that startled the secretary. When Banning departed, Mina went to investigate.

About forty feet from the office, where his victim's screams would not reach the stairwell, the killer brandished a claw hammer. Seeing the silvery glint of the metallic object, Mina Dekker made a futile attempt to defend herself. She clawed at her attacker's face, but he overpowered her and threw her to the floorboards. He stood over his dazed victim or knelt on her chest, pinning her to the floor.

As he raised the hammer, Mina instinctively threw up her right hand in a futile attempt to shield herself, but the hammer smashed through her right little finger and struck her in the temple. Her attacker swung the hammer four more times, the peen striking Dekker's scalp with the sound of a dull thud. The frenzied attack had to have left the assailant's clothes speckled with Mina Dekker's blood.

The killer could not know that Ray Peters would arrive at 1:30 p.m. and likely believed he had about half an hour before Charles and Robert Blackford returned from lunch. Either way, he would not need that much time. While Mina Dekker lay dying on the floorboards, her head in a halo of blood and the eerie silence of the stockroom broken by the gurgling sounds of her death rattle, the killer slipped on an overcoat, tucked the blood-streaked hammer into a pocket and raced down the steps (or alternately rode the freight elevator) to the first floor. A horse hair found at the scene, consistent with that used in suit coats, supports the idea that the killer wore a coat, but he may also have brought along a change of clothes or worn dark-colored clothes that would hide the specks of blood. He sneaked out of the building and disappeared.

Although all scenarios end up with Mina dying on the stockroom floor, there are a few possible, alternate preludes to the attack. The killer might have assumed the guise of a customer and, with the pretense of seeing an item or checking the availability of an item, lured Dekker into the warehouse—although in this scenario, he almost certainly entered the third-floor office from the front entrance and risked being seen by the Manufacturer's Supply Company employees.

Mina Dekker could have gone into the stockroom to investigate the noise she heard and found someone she knew, someone who wanted to talk her into, or out of, something. Their tête-à-tête turned into an argument that ended in a swift, frenzied attack.

During the investigation, police questioned everyone and anyone known to have seen Mina Dekker on March 4.

Charles and Robert Blackford lunched at the Pantlind Hotel until approximately 1:15 p.m., when they went their separate ways. Charles went to a local clothier to try on a new suit, while Robert went to Herpolsheimer's Department Store. They returned to Behr-Manning a few minutes after Ray Peters found their stenographer sprawled out on the floorboards of the stockroom.

The last person other than the killer to see Dekker alive, seventeen-year-old Herbert Banning, left the Western Union office at 12:46 p.m. to bring a message to the Behr-Manning office. He returned to Western Union three minutes later, at 12:49 p.m. Banning's account provided one end of the time frame for the murder. He did not see anyone when he left the Judd Building.

Ray Peters's discovery of Mina Dekker at 1:30 p.m. provided the other end of the time frame. Like Banning, Peters did not see a single soul when he entered the Judd Building. Still shaken, the shoemaker recounted his horrific discovery on the third floor. "While I was standing in the doorway," he said, "I heard someone moaning. I walked in the direction of the sound and just inside the stock room I saw her lying there."

Peters provided a detailed timeline of his movements on March 4. At 1:00 p.m., his father-in-law drove him to the license bureau, and from there he walked to Kresge five-and-dime on Monroe Avenue. After eating lunch, he headed to Behr-Manning, arriving at approximately 1:25 p.m.

The cobbler claimed to have never met Mina Dekker, but detectives found an eyewitness who told a curious story that suggested otherwise. The eyewitness—a customer who dropped in at Behr-Manning about a week before the murder—recalled seeing a man matching Peters's description leave the office. The man appeared to be grumbling about something. Once in the office, the customer found Mina Dekker in tears, and when he asked her what was wrong, she indicated that she had taken her shoes to the man who had just left the building. According to Marie Dekker, however, Mina always took her shoes to Monty's for repair and never once mentioned the name "Ray Peters." Investigators apparently did not think much about Peters as a suspect or this tantalizing anecdote, which never made it into the newspapers and exists only as a typewritten blurb in the notes of the original investigation.

Nevertheless, Peters became the unfortunate subject of a vicious rumor mill. Confounded by gossip and with his nerves frayed to the point of snapping, he requested a lie detector test to kill any lingering suspicions.

Chief O'Malley did his part in trying to squelch the rumors. "Peters has at no time been locked up for the murder of Mina Dekker," O'Malley said, "nor has he been under suspicion by this department. He has been the victim of vicious gossip and he wants to go to Lansing to take the lie detector test. We are glad to have him go for the results of this test may help check the idle tongues." Several times when speaking to the press, O'Malley alluded to the importance of avoiding the type of "vicious gossip" that had ensnared Ray Peters.

Arthur Leopold and Ray Coby spent the time between 12:50 p.m. and 1:30 p.m. in the office of the Manufacturer's Supply Company eating lunch and playing cards. Leopold said he might have heard a door slam, and Coby believed he heard the freight elevator operating at some point during that interval. At the time, it was debated if they could have heard sounds emanating from the freight entrance; their office was located at the front of the building, and both the door to the freight entrance and the freight elevator were located at the opposite side of the building.

The other Manufacturer's Supply Company employee, truck driver Calvin DeBlaey, returned from a delivery around 1:30 p.m., just before Peters ran into the office blathering about a bleeding and unconscious girl. He joined in the card game played by Leopold, Coby and Ira Dalyrymple, who worked in a nearby building but sometimes drifted over to the first-floor office, where he spent his lunch hour playing cards.

A Sunday school teacher at a local Christian Reformed Church, Calvin DeBlaey admitted knowing Dekker and talking to her on numerous occasions but insisted he knew nothing about the murder. The twenty-seven-year-old truck driver provided a detailed timeline of his movements on Friday, March 4. After making a delivery that afternoon, he returned to the office at 1:00 p.m. He opened the freight entrance door and sat on the freight elevator but decided to grab a cup of joe before going inside. "I heard of a nearby place that served a good cup of coffee so I decided to go there before returning to the office," DeBlaey explained. "I must have returned about 1:15 p.m. and sat down to a card game with some other fellows when Peters ran in and said he found a girl hurt upon the third floor."

On Friday night, Chief O'Malley interviewed Mina's former beau John Schafer. The nineteen-year-old college student had not seen Mina for several weeks and presented a rock-solid alibi for the afternoon of March 4. At about the same time that Herbert Banning entered the third floor of the Judd Building to pick up an outgoing message, Schafer was in class at the Heaney Commercial College. Several classmates verified his presence from 12:55 p.m. to 2:30 p.m., the crucial time frame in which Mina's murder occurred.

When presented with the notes found in Mina's purse—notes hinting at a relationship gone sour—Schafer said they were probably intended for him. "Those notes found in Mina's purse must have been meant for me," Schafer said. "If they had been sent, I would have gone to see her and our differences patched up."

Wiping tears from his eyes, Schafer provided the backstory. He and Mina had gone steady for about a year but had a cooling-off about a month earlier when she spotted him with someone else.

"We planned to be married as soon as I completed my course in school and got a job," he explained. "Mina was planning her hope chest and then suddenly she saw me with another girl and became jealous. That caused the quarrel which could have been patched up quickly, I am sure, if I received the notes."

Schafer believed he and Mina would have eventually reconciled. Distraught, he spent the days after Mina's death grieving with her family.

At the beginning of the investigation, O'Malley followed a line that either an insane pervert or a transient might have stalked the attractive secretary. Waiting for an opportune time, this person sneaked into the nearly deserted building and bludgeoned Mina Dekker.

"I am convinced that this crime was the work of a fiend," O'Malley declared at the outset of the investigation. "Without a visible motive we must proceed with that idea in mind. We are assuming for the present that the killer knew Miss Dekker was there alone during the noon hour. However, we are not overlooking the fact that the location is one which is frequented by transients." The proximity of a train station—across the street from the Judd Building—lent credence to the possibility that some deranged "transient" committed the crime and then hopped on a train and rode out of town.

The chief's theory led to a dragnet of the city's "vagrants and degenerates," but the subsequent grilling failed to churn up anything solid. Investigators searched every flophouse in the area for a blood-streaked claw hammer and blood-speckled clothes but came up empty-handed.

Just mentioning Mina Dekker's name put one man over the grill. It was testament to either the thoroughness or desperation of the police when they nabbed a suspected prowler and subjected him to intense questioning because, during his arrest, he mentioned the Dekker case.

O'Malley expressed his frustration with the lack of clues when he addressed the press on the eve of Mina Dekker's funeral service. "We are without a single thread of information to help us," O'Malley said. "Perhaps someone saw the killer flee the building where the girl was slain with a hammer. Or perhaps later someone saw a man wearing a blood-stained coat. If any such witness will call the police he may help materially in solving the brutal crime."

Inspector Albert Scheiern seconded the chief's comments. "Nothing has been found to date that will lead us to the slayer," Scheiern said before adding a provocative remark. "We have our opinions, but these we will keep to ourselves until we find something to go on."

Mina Dekker's funeral took place on Monday, March 7. She achieved a kind of postmortem notoriety common among murder victims. A *Grand Rapids Herald* writer described the scene: "One thousand persons, many of them curiosity seekers, crowded the church, filling every available seat and standing in rows around the walls, while at least 100 close friends and relatives accompanied the weeping mother and gray-haired father from the chapel to the church."

O'Malley, aware that his killer might attend the service and present some outward sign or gesture of his guilt, stationed plainclothes detectives in the pews with orders to observe anything out of the ordinary, such as an out-of-place smile or a smirk. But none of the thousand spectators tipped his hand with some incriminating tell. Although he was reticent about discussing the specifics with the press, the chief did have a prime suspect.

Calvin DeBlaey became a person of interest when detectives found minor inconsistencies in his statements and a suspicious gap in his timeline. After checking up on his movements, detectives could not locate witnesses to verify his whereabouts during the crucial period between 12:50 p.m.

and 1:30 p.m. And DeBlaey put himself at the freight elevator—almost certainly the killer's point of exit from the building—at 1:15 p.m.

Suspicions were further raised when Mina's sister Marie told police that Mina had complained about DeBlaey's demeanor, specifically the way he looked at and spoke to her. Detectives envisioned a scenario in which DeBlaey made advances to an unwilling Dekker, and when she threatened to go public with the harassment or tell his fiancée, he silenced her to protect his reputation. Chief O'Malley asked DeBlaey to take a polygraph.

On March 8—the day after Mina's funeral—detectives escorted Calvin DeBlaey to state police headquarters in East Lansing. The results were inconclusive. Contemporary accounts suggest that DeBlaey's frayed nerves led to a crying jag, which impeded the accuracy of the test.

Subsequent to the first lie detector test, DeBlaey made an admission, but not the confession that O'Malley and the other detectives anticipated. He fessed up to spending much of his lunch hour at the Uptown Recreation Parlor, where he engaged in an activity strictly forbidden by his church: playing cards for money. This part of DeBlaey's timeline checked out; fellow gamblers verified his presence at the Parlor until approximately 12:50 p.m. Detectives still could not find corroboration for DeBlaey's whereabouts from 12:50 p.m. until he showed up at the Manufacturer's Supply Company office at 1:30 p.m.

Two days later, DeBlaey sat for a second polygraph. During the test, he admitted to seeing Mina Dekker at 10:00 a.m. on the morning of the murder when he went to the third floor along with a customer. Again, the test results proved inconclusive. He fibbed about minor details but told the truth when he said he had nothing to do with the murder.

Nonetheless, Chief O'Malley decided to detain DeBlaey based on the results of the lie detector tests. "The experts at the state police laboratory felt that we should hold DeBlaey for further examination and so I locked him up," O'Malley told reporters before adding a caveat. "I most certainly do not want to cause any innocent person any suffering, yet at the same time, I cannot afford to take any chances."

O'Malley suggested a truth serum test, which DeBlaey adamantly refused to take. After consulting with his minister and discussing the matter with O'Malley and Kent County prosecutor Fred Searl, the truck driver eventually acquiesced. On Saturday, March 12, Calvin DeBlaey became the first murder suspect in Michigan to undergo such a test when Dr. L.M. Snyder, a medical consultant with the state police, injected him with scopolamine. The drug supposedly prevented the suspect from withholding information.

They asked DeBlaey questions such as "Did you use a club?" "Did you use a hammer?" and "Where did you hide your weapon?"

Under the influence of the "truth drug," the driver gave straightforward responses. Scopolamine, although today considered an unreliable means of ascertaining the truth, was DeBlaey's "get-out-of-jail" card in 1938. Prosecutor Fred Searl ordered his release from police custody on March 12 after, in the words of a *Herald* reporter, "the youth had clearly demonstrated… that he had not committed the crime."

Although the tests appeared to clear DeBlaey in 1938, suspicions about his possible involvement in the murder lingered for years and still surface whenever the Mina Dekker case is discussed.

Desperation on the part of investigators—or their thoroughness—was personified in the form of two suspects that emerged at the end of March. Detroit nabbed an eighteen-year-old man who had returned to the city shortly after the Dekker murder with scratches across his hands. The youngster periodically talked about the case, and these morbid inquiries eventually reached the ears of Detroit police, who contacted O'Malley.

O'Malley and Scheiern made the trip east and interviewed the kid but left convinced that he had nothing to do with the crime. He had a rock-solid alibi for March 4. He spent the day working at local farm, where he had obtained the scratches on his hands while handling cats.

A pair of trousers, along with a home address near the Judd Building, earned a local married man a one-night stay inside the Kent County Jail. The man, who lived near the crime scene, sent a pair of apparently blood-spotted trousers to a dry cleaner four days after the Dekker slaying. The blood came from an injured horse, and the man had an unshakeable alibi for March 4.

Three weeks into the investigation, O'Malley and Scheiern received a provocative clue. The night before her murder, Mina Dekker went to a shower for one of her dearest friends, Mary J. Kosten. Visibly agitated, she made several overtures about not wanting to walk home alone. She appeared preoccupied and uncharacteristically nervous, as if something preyed on her mind. She asked Kosten to walk home with her and promised to explain on the way, to "tell something terrible."

Kosten did not want to leave a party thrown in her honor, a decision she later came to regret. "I wish now that I had accompanied her," Kosten later told a *Grand Rapids Press* reporter. "If I knew what she wanted to tell me it might provide the solution to her death. I remember I received a postal card the day before from Mina saying she wanted to tell me something. I threw the card away." That "something terrible" and the fear that Mina felt the night before her murder indicated that Mina may have known her murderer.

Scheiern continued to run down clues as they periodically arose but failed to find the key to solving the Dekker enigma. The case files had collected a decade of dust when the *Grand Rapids Press* ran a front-page item on the tenth anniversary of the crime. Reflecting his undying hope for eventual closure, Scheiern commented, "Perhaps the murderer's conscience will one day force him to confess. In the meantime our men are still working on the case. If the murderer is still alive we may yet bring him to justice."

Another decade had passed when the *Grand Rapids Press* ran another front-page article to mark the twentieth anniversary of the murder mystery. "There is a long-shot chance," the unnamed reporter wrote, "a murderer will walk into Grand Rapids police headquarters next Tuesday, ready at last to tell his story. Why Tuesday? Because on that date Mina Dekker will have been dead for 20 years. The killer doubtless will be aware of the anniversary. Its occurrence may provide the impetus for an attempt, however late, to relieve a guilt-burdened conscience."

Tuesday, March 4, 1958, came and went without the revelatory confession. Without a confession or a belated break in the case, the murder of Mina Dekker would remain unsolved, although some members of the original investigation had more than an inkling about where the finger of blame should point.

Speaking of the case on the eve of his retirement in 1959, Detective Frank Breen remarked, "I am completely convinced in my own mind that I know the identity of the person who killed her. I am as certain of it as I am that my name is Frank Breen. But because of certain peculiar circumstances which I cannot divulge here, it has been impossible so far to accumulate enough evidence against this person to assure a conviction."

"Her case has not been," he added, "and never should be, marked closed until her slayer is dead, or behind bars."

The how, what, where and when of the crime were established during the 1938 investigation, but the who and the why remain unknowns. The sheer brutality of the crime, however, may be suggestive of the why. The fatal wounds—not one, not two, but five hammer blows—hint at the personal nature of the killer's still-unidentified motive.

Why, if any one of the hammer blows would have killed Mina Dekker, did her killer strike her five times when the castoff stains would have left him covered in blood? Perhaps not realizing the lethality of the first blow, he continued to hit her so she could never finger him as her slayer. Perhaps out of fear, mercy or a desire to ensure his victim's death, the killer administered a coup de grâce with four additional hammer blows. Or he panicked.

There is another possibility that is even more suggestive of motive. The viciousness of the murder hints at an underlying rage that emanated from some deep, personal affront—the type of rage often associated with affaires de coeur, such as love triangles, unrequited love and women scorned. The sheer savagery of the murder, not unlike that of the Grace Loomis case, suggested a crime of passion rather than a crime of opportunity or an assassination. The murderer did not just want to kill Mina Dekker; he wanted to destroy her, which would explain why he struck her five times, pulping her skull with a claw hammer and leaving him coated in her blood.

Contemporary news sources played up Dekker's image as a choir singer, a one-man woman raised by parents who viewed smoking, drinking and cinema as three deadly sins, but did the "something terrible" that Mina wanted to divulge on the eve of her murder involve some sort of romantic entanglement? If she became a married man's "other woman," then at least one possible motive for her murder comes into focus. If such a tryst resulted in a pregnancy, then an equally viable motive emerges. Could the hammer have come down to flatten a love triangle? Investigators must have pondered something along this line; according to the original investigation notes in the case file, an examination "for signs of pregnancy" was conducted on Mina Dekker's body at the funeral home on the evening of March 4, 1938, and a postmortem done "for that purpose that evening."

If Mina had such an entanglement, however, she hid it well. None of the people in her personal orbit reported any such relationship, but then again, she may have blanched at divulging information about something she considered shameful, embarrassing or even scandalous.

Perhaps a more likely scenario has Mina Dekker as the object of an obsession, the recipient of unwanted and relentless advances or the victim of a stalker who made the ultimate "If I cannot have her, no one can" statement with a hammer. Or she grew tired of his harassment and threatened to take her complaints to the authorities, or worse, the man's wife or partner, and so he silenced her before she had the chance.

It is equally possible that Dekker was the victim of a sexual assault, the knowledge of which posed a serious threat to the perpetrator. If this was Dekker's "something terrible," then perhaps her murderer silenced her before she had a chance to say a word. This scenario would also explain the postmortem search "for signs of pregnancy." Maybe Dekker believed, and her killer feared, that he had impregnated her.

A series of letters that disappeared after Mina Dekker's murder may have contained vital clues about a tryst or an obsession gone awry. According to the investigation report in the case file, Detectives Anning and Taylor returned to the Behr-Manning office on March 7 to search for letters "which were said to cause her [Mina Dekker] concern." The detectives left empty-handed, but these letters, if they in fact existed, may have shed some light on a motive for her murder.

The case of Mina Dekker's murder—a riddle wrapped in a mystery inside an enigma—remains unsolved eighty years later. Perhaps buried somewhere deep in the original case records, a brown accordion file bulging with yellowing papers, lies the key that will someday unveil who killed her and why. Maybe closure will come in the form of a confession, a perimortem attempt to clear a troubled conscience, jotted on a scrap of paper and deposited in an old trunk.

The Usual Suspects

The Slaying of Senator Warren Hooper
(Lansing, 1945)

I t was the summer of 1943. Smiling for the camera, eleven men in white
shirts gathered around a red roadster, squinting in the bright sunshine
of a hot summer day, on the front lawn of Deputy Warden D.C. Pettit's
home. Four of the men sat in the vehicle, as if ready to motor away on a long
drive through the countryside, while the other seven stood around them in
various poses. One man—Raymond Fox—stood in the foreground, his hand
on his hip and his leg propped on the car's running board. Serving life for
armed robbery, Fox worked as a clerk in Pettit's office.

All convicted felons serving lengthy sentences for rape, murder and armed
robbery, these men represented a who's who of organized crime. They
"escaped" their hot cells inside the Jackson State Penitentiary to celebrate
the nuptials of the warden's son. Ted Pizzino, one of only three men who
did not wear a tie, looked away from the camera. Pizzino, who beat the rap
for the Buckley assassination, was in the fifteenth year of his sentence for
the gangland murder of William Cannon. The tall man in the back, Henry
Luks, grinned as he stared directly into the camera's eye.

The photograph became a key element in one of the state's most infamous
unsolved murders and came to symbolize the rampant corruption behind
one of the state's most infamous murders. While GIs island-hopped through
the Pacific, trading bullets with the Japanese as they went, the headlines in
January 1945 belonged to the investigation into the murder of State Senator
Warren G. Hooper.

At about 4:00 p.m. on Thursday, January 11, 1945, the sun had already begun to drop below the western horizon when forty-year-old Senator Warren G. Hooper motored out of Lansing.

Hooper casually sucked on a cigarette while he headed south on M-99 toward his home in Albion. He had traveled twenty-four miles from Lansing when, a few miles north of Springport and the Eaton County line, a car, which an eyewitness later described as "maroon," pulled alongside the senator's vehicle. The driver jerked the steering wheel to the right, and Hooper veered to avoid a collision. His car skidded to a stop at the left side of the road. The second car pulled in front of it, the two cars forming a T.

Hooper sat behind the wheel, stunned, as the driver's side door swung open and a man shoved him toward the passenger's seat. The man tugged Hooper's fedora down over his eyes, leveled his Colt .38 and squeezed the trigger four times. One bullet missed entirely, passing through the senator's hat and piercing the back window. Three bullets struck him in the head at point-blank range. One bullet passed through the skull behind his left ear. Another entered under his left eye at a downward angle and ended up in his throat. A third entered the top of his cranium, tore through his brain and came to a stop against his right shoulder blade. Hooper slumped to the right, and the cigarette dropped from his lips.

The assassin eyed his victim for a few seconds before climbing back into the idling vehicle. The "maroon" car peeled away as Hooper's lit cigarette began to smolder.

By the time a passing motorist stopped to investigate Hooper's car at about 5:45 p.m., the smoldering cigarette had turned into a conflagration. The raging miniature inferno in the front seat had burned the entire length of Hooper's torso. The flames had licked at the fingers of Hooper's hands, exposing the phalanges.

Three passersby pulled Hooper's charred body from the vehicle and then began tossing handfuls of snow into the car to check the blaze. A few minutes later, firefighters arrived on the scene and extinguished the remaining embers. Within the hour, a team of investigators began to comb the scene for clues.

Apart from the .38 bullet later removed from Hooper's skull, the assassin had left behind one provocative clue: small shoe prints leading away from the driver's side of Hooper's automobile. The impressions in the snow—made by about a five- or a five-and-a-half-sized shoe—suggested that a small-statured man or possibly a woman made the hit.

Investigators did not have to search far for a motive. The forty-year-old legislator was in his first term as a state senator after having served three terms as a representative. A native of Los Angeles, California, Hooper came to Albion, Michigan, in 1929, where he worked as an advertising manager at the *Albion Evening Recorder*. In 1936, he married Calienetta Cobb, and together they had two sons.

In 1938, Hooper successfully ran for the Michigan House of Representatives. He won reelection in 1940 and again in 1942. In 1944, Hooper won the state senate seat from the Ninth District, representing Branch and Calhoun Counties.

Hooper became a prime mover in a grand jury sweep of corrupt legislators and their backers. The one-man grand jury of Judge Leland W. Carr, aided by Special Investigator (and later Governor) Kim Sigler, handed down dozens of indictments, which by the time of the Hooper assassination had already netted twenty convictions.

In exchange for immunity from prosecution, Hooper became a key witness in the case against three men who stood accused of using bribes in an attempt to kill the "pari-mutuel betting bill" or "racing bill": Frank D. McKay, a business scion from Grand Rapids; Floyd Fitzsimmons, a sports promotor from Benton Harbor; and William Green, a former legislator from Hillman. Hooper also planned to testify against William J. Burns, the executive secretary of the Michigan State Medical Society, who faced trial for attempting to bribe lawmakers into passing some medical legislation. Hooper testified that Burns offered him an all-expenses-paid vacation to California in exchange for his help.

It appeared that someone on the grand jury's hit list attempted to bully the state's witnesses with threats of violence. One witness claimed that he had been offered hush money to leave the country or else. Another claimed that two men in a black sedan threatened to kill him if he did not develop a quick case of amnesia. Hooper may have received similar threats of violence or promises of monetary gifts if he suddenly turned mute.

Sigler may have felt that the grand jury investigation was cursed. In the previous month, several witnesses had died in horrific accidents. In December, the operator of a transportation company under investigation for alleged graft died ironically when a train t-boned his car. That same month, State Senator Earl Wright Munshaw was found dead in the garage on his Kent County farm just two days after giving testimony to Carr's grand jury. The coroner ruled Munshaw's death by carbon monoxide poisoning an accident.

Sigler, apparently aware of the danger to his key witnesses, offered Hooper police protection, but the senator refused, apparently believing that a bodyguard trailing him around the capital would be embarrassing. His denial led, tragically, to the smoldering ruins of a car on a lonely stretch of M-99 and a toe tag.

State Police Chief Oscar Olander coordinated a massive manhunt for Hooper's assassins, while several newspapers offered sizable cash rewards for information. Special Prosecutor Kim Sigler joined the investigation into the murder of his key witness, a man he characterized as his "little bundle of dynamite." With Sigler's "dynamite" buried, the case against McKay, Fitzsimmons and Green appeared over before it had begun.

The first of two major breaks in the case came on January 13, when an eyewitness emerged. Harry Snyder, a motorist who passed the scene just seconds after the shooting, told an intriguing story.

Snyder slowed his vehicle when he noticed a maroon car, a 1941 or 1942 model, blocking the highway ahead. He spotted one man behind the wheel and another standing next to the open door of Hooper's car. He also saw a figure slumped over in the front seat. As Snyder neared, the driver of the maroon car pulled to the side of the road. Both men stared at Snyder as he slowly motored past. From his rearview mirror, Snyder watched as the second man jumped into the maroon car, his path coinciding with the smallish footprints found at the scene. The incident, Snyder said, occurred at precisely 5:30 p.m.

Two clues emerged from Snyder's statement: Hooper's assassin followed a well-orchestrated plan, and he wore small shoes.

The second major breakthrough in the case came in March, when two ex-cons—Henry (Heine) Luks and Sam Abramowitz—turned state's evidence. The break came from a letter to Leland Carr penned by Alfred "Al" Kurner, who said that two men—Mike Selik and Harry Fleisher—offered him $5,000 to bump off a prominent politician. Kurner also said that Selik and Fleisher made similar offers to Luks and Abramowitz.

Henry Luks, who met Selik while doing time in the State Prison at Jackson, was an influential convict who even attended a social gathering at Assistant Deputy Warden Pettit's house and stood at the center of a group photograph taken on Pettit's front lawn. A self-described "three-time loser," Luks was serving four and a half to ten years for a third offense when the unnamed photographer snapped the picture of the grinning jailbirds on the lawn of Pettit's house in 1943.

According to Luks, known Purple Gang associates Myron (Mike) Selik and Harry Fleisher offered him and Sam Abramowitz $5,000 to participate

Three goodfellas and a lawman. *From left to right*: Purple Gang associate Irving Milberg, Purple Gang chief Raymond Bernstein (*smiling at the photographer*), Purple Gang associate Harry Keywell (*back to the camera*) and Wayne County sheriff Edward Behrendt (*sitting to the left of Bernstein*). *Walter P. Reuther Library, Archives of Labor and Urban Affairs, Wayne State University.*

Wise guys: Harry Fleisher (*left*) photographed with Myron Selik in 1945. *Walter P. Reuther Library, Archives of Labor and Urban Affairs, Wayne State University.*

in a hit on an important witness. Selik and Fleisher did not name the target, and Abramowitz only learned the man's identity much later. The four men traveled to Albion to reconnoiter the job on December 26, 1944.

Prior to this, Luks said, Selik visited Purple Gang kingpins Raymond Bernstein and Harry Keywell inside the State Prison at Jackson ostensibly with the purpose of plotting the murder. Luks detailed the various methods envisioned for the hit. They planned to booby-trap Hooper's car with explosives, but he could not get dynamite. Another plan had Abramowitz distracting the mark and Luks hitting him in the head and then garroting him with a necktie. Luks ultimately decided to quit the job because he thought it "was too hot," which left Abramowitz to carry out the contract.

Sam Abramowitz, a career criminal with two prison convictions and by his own count over one hundred arrests, also turned state's evidence and agreed to turn on Selik and Fleisher in exchange for immunity from prosecution. Judge and one-man grand jury Leland Carr agreed to the deal.

Abramowitz corroborated much of what Luks said. He confessed to accepting a contract from Selik and Fleisher to kill an unnamed witness. Harry Fleisher, he said, told him the hit would be worth $15,000, although he did not know who was paying the tab.

After Luks walked away from the job, Abramowitz and Harry Fleisher's brother Sam, who would act as the getaway driver, returned to Albion on two separate occasions. They came closest to carrying out the contract during the second trip, on January 2, 1945. Abramowitz planned to walk up to the target and put two .38 slugs in his chest but aborted the plot at the last minute when he spotted a woman and two children in Hooper's office.

Fed up, he decided he too would drop out of the conspiracy and broke the news to Harry Fleisher. "I said I was dropping out; I was not going back to Albion a third time," Abramowitz later testified. "That is when Harry said, 'I guess Mike and I will do it ourselves.'"

The bombshell testimony of Luks and Abramowitz led to charges against Harry and Sam Fleisher, Myron (Mike) Selik and Peter Mahoney for conspiracy to commit murder.

The trial of the conspirators opened amid a heat wave in July 1945. Both Luks and Abramowitz stuck to the stories they told to investigators and repeated at the preliminary hearing. Selik and Harry Fleisher hired them to assassinate an important witness, they testified, and Sam Fleisher drove Abramowitz in his brother's black Pontiac in an aborted attempt to carry out the contract.

Not until much later did the hit men learn the identity of their mark. Their employers were cagey about naming names. "Henry Luks asked Selik if the fellow had anything to do with that grand jury at Lansing," Abramowitz testified. "Luks asked him if it had anything to do with that man named McKay. Selik told him to pay no attention to that part of it, that there had been $16,000 put up for the job and that was all we needed to know."

The would-be hit man described lying in wait for the senator in Albion, the scheme thwarted by the presence of a woman. "I saw him (the victim) from the top of his shoulders up. He was leaning back as though his head was resting on the window and he was pretty bald," the witness recalled. "Sam Fleisher said it looked to him as if someone was sitting across the desk from Hooper and I said yes, it was a woman. As we drove slowly by the office, we saw kids playing in the building. Sam said that was Mrs. Hooper. We drove around and thought maybe she would leave. We thought it would be a bad time to do anything with the woman and the kids there."

According to the state's star witness, the motive behind Hooper's assassination was his upcoming testimony before Carr's grand jury into graft. "I was told by all three," Abramowitz recalled on the stand, "that there was a time limit on the deal—that if Hooper wasn't killed by the next Thursday that he would be able to talk before the grand jury."

Abramowitz repeated the damning statement that appeared to implicate Selik and Harry Fleisher as the shooters in Hooper's assassination. "I asked Harry and Mike if there was a chance of making any more trips to Albion," he testified. "Harry said, 'No,' and added that he and Selik would take care of it themselves." While Selik and Fleisher were on trial as middlemen and not triggermen, this statement hinted that one or both may have played a more active role in the actual shooting.

Abramowitz's credibility, and shoe size, became the focal points during his cross-examination by defense attorney Maurice J. Walsh. The thirty-six-year-old witness had spent most of his adult life behind bars. His first prison sentence stemmed from a 1928 conviction for breaking and entering. He did another, lengthier stint for an armed robbery conviction in 1936, emerging from the State Prison at Jackson in 1943.

In addition to Abramowitz's shady credibility, the shoe fit, literally. He wore a size eight, he admitted, which fit the size of the shoeprints leading away from Hooper's smoldering automobile. But he said he spent January 11 in Flint and only heard of the murder that evening. Abramowitz's alibi did not prevent defense attorney Edward H. Kennedy Jr. from alleging that he may have pulled the trigger himself.

Although Sigler's case depended on two career criminals, whose testimony consisted of bits and pieces of rehashed conversations, the jury took just two hours to return a verdict of guilty against all four defendants. Rather than the typical tears, the four men grinned when they listened to the sentence of four and a half to five years. Convicted on the flimsiest of hearsay evidence, Mahoney could not believe his ears. The court later overturned his conviction.

Kim Sigler expressed his belief in the eventual solution to the Hooper murder mystery in his victory remarks to the press. "This is the opening wedge in the solution of the Hooper murder case," he gloated. Sigler also touched on the credibility issues of Luks and Abramowitz, calling the verdict "a complete vindication of the witnesses of the state, particularly those who had criminal records."

Over seventy-five years have passed since the Hooper jury returned a verdict of guilty, and the "opening wedge" has failed to reveal either the triggerman or the moneyman behind the Hooper assassination.

According to Henry Luks, the murder of Warren Hooper was preceded by a meeting between Harry Fleisher and jailed underworld bosses Harry Keywell and Raymond Bernstein inside the State Prison at Jackson. The alleged gathering, conducted with the knowledge if not the blessing of prison officials, raised the specter of an in-house cabal of powerful crime lords who continued to call the shots from the inside. It also suggested the possibility that Selik and Fleisher may have contracted hit men from the prison population.

While the Hooper conspiracy trial unfolded in Battle Creek, Attorney General John Dethmers conducted a probe into corruption inside the prison. The investigation resulted in part from the case of Joseph Medley, a convict who simply walked out. While free, he murdered two women. The Medley case created an outcry and led to an official inquiry into not only the laxity of prison administration but also the possibility of an inner sanctum of hoods running the show inside the prison.

Dethmers released his report in late July 1945, at about the midway point in the conspiracy trial. The timing chafed Kim Sigler, who accused the attorney general of grandstanding for personal political gain. In his report, Dethmers suggested the surreal possibility of contract killers slipping out of their cells to make the hit on Hooper and then slipping back in again with the perfect alibi. While investigators hunted the shooters, they were behind bars of a state penitentiary.

The almost-smoking gun, Dethmers suggested in his report, consisted of a clandestine meeting of criminal minds that occurred sometime before the Hooper assassination. "Shortly prior to that time Selik and other known Purple gangsters were permitted by Chief Inspector Walter L. Wilson to visit known gangsters (Purples) who were in Jackson Prison, and permitted a private interview," Dethmers wrote. "It is a known fact that inmates have been away from the prison although still 'on count.'"

Dethmers did the math. Luks and Abramowitz pulled out of the contract. Selik and Fleisher, who said they would take care of business themselves, visited Keywell and Bernstein in prison. The attorney general gave a rundown of the Murder, Inc-arcerated theory:

> *This gives rise to the question as to whether it is not possible that Selik and Fleisher were able to contact one or more gangsters who are doing time for murder at the present time, arrange to take them away from the prison to commit the murder and return to the prison in sufficient time to leave them with a perfect alibi; that is, of being confined in the Southern*

Michigan Prison and "on count" at the time the murder took place. When asked whether this was possible, Director Garrett Heyns of the Corrections Commission answered "yes."

It was not an entirely far-fetched scenario. Dethmers identified a "prison-control ring" led by ten inmates who supposedly left the prison to attend parties and shows in Jackson and baseball games in Detroit. They even hosted parties at a prison official's cottage. The key figures of the "ring" were Henry Luks, Mike Selik, Joseph Medley and seven others.

The attorney general uncovered another link between Selik and his former prison-mates: a pipeline bringing whiskey from O'Larry's Bar, where Selik and Fleisher concocted the plan to assassinate Hooper, into the prison.

Among other revelations, the attorney general's report contained the story of a prisoner's wife who became pregnant after visiting her husband in the prison hospital. A one-dollar tip to the attendant purchased privacy screens positioned around the hospital bed. The anecdote pulled the curtains back to reveal the real purpose of the infirmary, which one journalist described as "a cupid's bower used regularly as a place of assignation for convicts with their wives or sweethearts."

Warden Harry Jackson's response was equal parts shock and indignation. Referring to the incident in which inmates, including Henry Luks, attended a wedding party at Deputy Pettit's house, Jackson said, "They went, not as guests, but to help with arrangements."

If the State Prison at Jackson was a "playhouse" for powerful gangsters, Dethmers's probe led to a timeout for two of its key players. Bernstein and Keywell, both serving life sentences for their role in the infamous Collingwood Manor Massacre, were sent to the State Prison in Marquette, about as far away as possible from their underworld connections in Detroit.

The graft case against Frank McKay collapsed after Hooper's murder. Sigler subsequently prosecuted him on a charge of violating state liquor laws, but McKay beat the rap. His co-defendants did not fare as well. Convicted of graft in attempting to sway legislators in the racing bill, Fitzsimmons spent four years in prison; Green went down for a different bribery charge.

After serving a term as governor and then losing his reelection bid, Kim Sigler continued to pursue the puppeteer pulling the strings of the Hooper assassination. He remained convinced that Fleisher and Selik held the key to solving the murder, so he devised a way to loosen their tongues. He brought charges against Fleisher, Selik and three other men in the armed robbery of the Aristocrat Club with the idea that they would be more likely to make a deal if they faced lengthy prison sentences.

Sigler achieved half of his goal. A jury convicted the men, who subsequently jumped bail. They remained on the lam for over a year. Police found Selik hiding out in New York, while federal authorities nabbed Fleisher on a Florida beach. Neither man, however, provided Sigler with closure in the Hooper case.

The Dethmers scenario received support in an intriguing twist that occurred in November 1949, when Mitchell Bonkowski and Herman Faubert, two inmates of the State Prison at Jackson, came forward with a story that appeared to solve the case. According to Faubert, the conspirators cooked up the assassination plot in the house of Deputy Warden Pettit.

Flaubert provided a narrative of the crime. Selik, who attempted to bribe Hooper, left Lansing in the senator's car. The plotters hoped that Selik could silence Hooper by coaxing him into accepting a sizable cash bribe, and if he failed, they would silence the senator with bullets. Faubert, Morris Rader, Dale Mazaroff and Ben Lobadie followed in two cars while John Johnson waited in a truck at a prearranged ambush site.

When Hooper refused the $25,000 bribe, Selik stopped the car. Rader and Mazaroff jumped out and shot Hooper with a .38 supplied by Faubert. The conspirators bivouacked at Pettit's house, where they split the $25,000, buried the pistol and parted company.

Rader and Mazaroff denied playing any part in the assassination. Because the story changed slightly with each telling, state police used lie detector tests in an attempt to sift fact from fiction. Detroit police commissioner Harry S. Toy, convinced by the new account of Hooper's murder, described the outcome of the polygraphs. "Bonkowski and Faubert were telling the truth," he proclaimed.

A squad of detectives combed Pettit's property for the missing .38, supposedly buried in a plumbing trench, but they came up empty-handed. Nonetheless, Toy proclaimed the Hooper case solved.

A month later, in December 1949, Flaubert made another admission: his plot to murder Hooper occurred nowhere but in his own mind. He made up the story in a failed play for a parole.

A few books and endless conjecture have filled the seventy-five years since the Hooper assassination, but despite the best efforts of detectives—both official and armchair—the case remains unsolved. With a tip of the hat to John Dethmers and the possibility that Selik may have contracted a prisoner to make the hit, the shoe (both literally and figuratively) might fit one of three Cinder-fellas.

During the trial, Edward H. Kennedy made no bones about the possibility that one of the state's star witnesses—Sam Abramowitz— shot Hooper. Kennedy also made much of the fact that Abramowitz had traded information for immunity, which meant that Leland Carr and Kim Sigler had let him off the hook. This made his clients the scapegoats for a politically charged investigation. However, except for the fact that Abramowitz's shoe size roughly fit the tracks leading away from Hooper's car, there was nothing tying him to the murder. He had an alibi that put him in Flint on January 11, 1945.

Abramowitz's testimony suggested that either Selik or Fleisher pulled the trigger while the other waited in the getaway vehicle, but again, the only "evidence" remains one piece of hearsay uttered by a career criminal.

In the Hooper case, all roads may just lead back to the State Prison at Jackson, both literally and figuratively. The ambush occurred near the spot where the M-99 converges with the M-50, which leads to Jackson. Selik's alleged meeting with Bernstein and Keywell during the planning stages of the murder hints at involvement of the high-ranking Purples, both of whom had a history of violent homicide (both were serving life sentences for their roles in the Collingwood Manor Massacre of 1931). And a maroon roadster mysteriously kept cropping up during the investigation, a car similar in appearance to Assistant Deputy Warden Pettit's vehicle—the prop used by the smiling convicts for the photo-op on Pettit's front lawn in 1943. Eleven convicts grinning like Cheshire cats.

Senator Warren G. Hooper's bullet-riddled hat resides in the Michigan State History Museum in Lansing, a tangible reminder of one of Michigan's most vexing unsolved crimes.

8

The Riddle of Lydia Thompson

(Detroit, 1945)

Imaginative Detroit newspapermen dubbed it the "Lover's Lane Murder," and for a week in 1945, news of the grisly slaying captivated the reading public. The discovery of mutilated remains along a remote dirt road in Oakland County pulled detectives into a Bermuda Love Triangle formed by a prosperous car salesman, his wife and his other woman.

According to *Detroit Times* reporter Elmer Williams, the bizarre story made better reading than anything imagined by Raymond Chandler or Dashiell Hammett. "No writer of fiction, weaving in his imagination a tale of society murder and intrigue," Williams wrote in his October 21 page-one story, "could have presented Detroit a mystery more baffling than the unsolved slaying of Mrs. Lydia Thompson, Russian-born businesswoman....Here...is the pattern and background of the perfect mystery novel—waiting only the final hour of denouement."

On Saturday afternoon, October 13, 1945, a mushroom picker stumbled across something in the tall grass along the edge of a path that branched off Ormond Road. Closer inspection revealed a ghastly sight: the mutilated remains of a woman. An ear-to-ear gash across her throat had nearly decapitated her, leaving her head connected to her torso by just a few sinews.

The victim wore a thick brown coat over a black pantsuit and one shoe containing a label from the J.L. Hudson Co. The other shoe, along with a blood-soaked maroon hat and a pair of black gloves, lay a few feet away from the body. The coat was damp, which suggested that the murderer probably dumped Jane Doe's body sometime before the previous Thursday, when a heavy rain had blanketed the area.

Oakland County sheriff deputies combed the nearby woods for clues. They failed to find the murder weapon—believed to be an axe or possibly a machete—but a blood-smeared depression in the dirt shoulder of the road suggested that the killer or killers dumped the unidentified victim's body from an automobile and then dragged it by the ankles down the path and out of sight. For whatever reason—harried by the thought of a chance discovery, exhausted by the frenetic attack and by dragging his victim—the killer left the body just a stone's throw from the edge of a swamp, which would have made an ideal place to deep-six the corpse. This suggested that the "Hatchet Fiend" did not know the lay of the land.

Locals knew the seldom-traveled Ormond Road as a "lover's lane," so police followed a line that an amorous encounter somehow went bad, evolving into a spat or quarrel and ending in a frenzied attack. Ravenous reporters, always hungry for a juicy story, seized on the initial theory of a lover's spat turned deadly and dubbed Jane Doe "The Lover's Lane Victim" and her killer "The Hatchet Fiend." Detroit's latest murder mystery debuted under a margin-to-margin front-page headline in the *Detroit Free Press*: "Hatchet Fiend Kills Woman."

The sheer brutality of the crime became evident during the postmortem. The cause of death was clear enough; Jane Doe exsanguinated when a heavy-bladed device sliced through her jugular and carotid. But Jane Doe's blouse hid a sinister secret.

Oakland County coroner Dr. Leon Cobb unbuttoned Jane Doe's blouse and discovered four deep stab wounds in her stomach, two of which perforated the abdominal wall, along with a series of thirteen small, antemortem perforations running the length of her torso. Caused by a thin-bladed weapon like an icepick, stiletto or penknife, the punctures showed evidence of healing, which indicated that an unspecified length of time— possibly even four or five days—had elapsed between these wounds and that fatal gash that left Jane Doe's head dangling from a string. This finding led Dr. Cobb to conclude that some as-yet-unidentified "sex maniac" or sadist tortured Jane Doe for several days before slashing her throat and dumping her almost headless body along a lonely stretch of country road.

He believed the wounds suggested a time frame for the crime: five days before Jane Doe's death, her killer repeatedly jabbed her with an icepick, causing thirteen painful but not fatal perforations. Three days later, he stabbed her with a bigger blade, causing the four deeper yet still nonfatal wounds. Two days after that, sometime during the evening of Thursday, October 11, he concluded his sadistic charade with something like an axe or a meat cleaver.

According to Dr. Cobb, the forensic evidence suggested a lengthy, drawn-out death and tended to refute the idea of a frenzied attack as first believed. A trail of blood from Ormond Road to the spot of discovery, coupled with tire tracks, indicated that the killer backed his car up to the path and dragged the body to the spot where he dumped it. The relative absence of blood anywhere near the body indicated the murder took place somewhere else.

Oddly, Jane Doe's clothing contained no rips, tears or punctures corresponding with the wounds, which suggested that the killer dressed her corpse.

In life, the woman—an attractive thirty- to thirty-five-year-old brunette with a pie-shaped face—weighed about 130 pounds, stood five feet, six inches tall and had blue eyes and manicured fingernails. An incision across her lower abdomen indicated that at one time, she had undergone a Caesarean section.

Over the next few days, detectives desperately tried to put a name with the pie-shaped face. Dozens of people viewed the body, but no one could identify her. Detectives from Windsor, who wondered if Jane Doe was the latest victim in a string of knifings that had terrorized their community, concluded that they followed a wild goose and left the morgue no closer to unmasking their culprit.

The corpse looked good for her age. In life, detectives learned, "Jane Doe" went by the name of Lydia Thompson and was the forty-seven-year-old estranged wife of a prosperous car dealer named Louis V. Thompson. An eyewitness saw Lydia alive at the couple's postmodern mansion in Orchard Lake around dusk on Thursday, October 11, which put the murder at about 8:30 p.m. that night. What happened during that three-hour interval remains a mystery to this day.

On the day she died, Lydia Thompson's movements appeared highly suspect, even bizarre. Shortly before 1:00 p.m., she went to a Highland Park grocery store, where she knew the owner, Avedis Hovanesian. While paying for her groceries, she fished through her purse and pulled out a small fragment of paper. Highly agitated, even panic-stricken, she begged Hovanesian to find the man whose name appeared on the paper. He was busy but suggested she return later.

"But you've got to do it," Lydia begged. Then she made the first in a series of ominous statements she would make that day. "I'm scared to death. I've got to know this—you've got to find this man for me." Hovanesian glanced at the piece of paper, handed it back to his customer and repeated his suggestion that she return later, at a slower time in the afternoon. Thompson reluctantly agreed and hurried out of the store.

A photograph of Lydia Thompson taken shortly before her death in 1945. *Author's collection.*

From the grocery, Lydia went to visit Harriet Steele, a longtime friend, who later described the odd encounter. In near hysterics, Lydia said she feared for her life. She had even bought a gun, she said, which she kept in her purse. When Steele asked her what was wrong, Lydia once again pulled the slip of paper from her purse and offered the cryptic remark, "Everything that causes this is on this slip of paper." She shoved the note back in her purse without showing it to Steele.

"Are you just crying about Vic," Steele asked, "or is it something else?"

"It's about something else entirely," Lydia replied. "I have a man's name on this slip of paper, and if I don't find out who he is right now, maybe I will not see you tomorrow."

Lydia briefly visited with another friend in Highland Park before going to Western Union and sending a cable to her birthplace of Rostov-on-Don in the Russian Ukraine at approximately 4:30 p.m.

Around dusk, an Orchard Park patrolman drove past the Thompson residence, where he saw Lydia Thompson chatting with a man and woman, although it was too dark, and he was too distant, to see anything but shapes. He was the last person to see Lydia Thompson alive.

A small legion of detectives scoured every inch of the Thompson estate, nestled along the edge of Orchard Lake, for the telltale bloodstains that would indicate the torture-murder took place inside the residence. Nothing appeared to suggest even the slightest struggle had occurred. No overturned chairs, no missing jewelry, no blood spatter.

And no .32 revolver. Lydia Thompson had purchased the weapon the previous August and attempted to obtain a permit to carry it because, she said, unidentified "prowlers" had pestered her at her Orchard Lake home. The missing weapon, Sheriff Thomas believed, would provide the key to solving Lydia Thompson's murder.

In the sewing room, detectives found a clue: draped over a chair was the maroon dress she wore on the afternoon of Thursday, October 11. Detectives believed that Lydia changed into work clothes she used to do chores around the house, and this fact indicated that she did not plan to leave the house. They followed a line that a prowler waited outside for her to change and then nabbed her, driving her to her death in her own vehicle.

Another provocative clue came in the form of a lined piece of paper containing a note. Penned in Russian and apparently in Lydia's handwriting, the note was addressed "Dear Father" and said he should "look for a man named Perrone who owns a gas station on E. Jefferson if anything happens to me." The note also contained a bequest: "Everything that belongs to me, according to the law, I leave to you, father."

The searches did not find a smoking-gun piece of evidence like a blood-smeared machete, but they did not come away empty-handed, either. The most tantalizing bit of evidence was an ordinary kitchen calendar containing a number of extraordinary notations. Apparently, Lydia Thompson had used it as a sort of diary and inked a series of entries, in Russian, in the blank spaces under each date. Some of the entries appeared coded, while others appeared to form a sequence of events.

In the week following the discovery of Lydia Thompson's body, clues continued to appear in the most unlikely of places. Detectives found her car in a Pontiac parking lot eighteen miles away from Grass Lake. A woman who used the same lot told police that she did not see Thompson's vehicle when she parked her car at 4:00 p.m. on Thursday, October 11, but did notice it when she returned at about 11:30 p.m. She noticed somebody moving about inside the car but could not tell if it was one or two people. She returned two hours later—at 1:30 a.m.—and the car was still there but deserted. Missing from the car: Lydia's purse, keys and .32 revolver.

"Oh, my God," Lydia wrote in one entry, "for all his dirty deeds, I still love him, love him without end." The entries in the large kitchen calendar formed a diary of sorts, which told a tragic chronicle of a middle-aged woman keenly aware of her fading beauty and the devolution of a marriage to a man she deeply loved.

The Thompsons' storybook romance began three decades earlier and half a world away from Orchard Lake when Lydia Andreyevna, a nurse and the widow of a White Russian soldier, met a dashing British soldier by the name of Louis Victor Thompson in Constantinople. They married in 1922.

A few years later, the newlyweds planted roots in the Detroit area, where Louis opened a car dealership. Business boomed, and the Thompsons built a mansion on Orchard Lake. The opulent house included a basement bar with red leather–upholstered chairs, an indoor swimming pool, a billiard room and a master bedroom with a walk-in closet stuffed with pricy dresses and lingerie. The couple also acquired a small building housing a laundry on the first floor and an apartment above it.

The diary entries take up the story beginning in January, the first month on the 1945 calendar. Although the Thompson marriage may have hit the rocks earlier, the first real sign of trouble in the diary appeared in a February entry, when Lydia describes an incident when "Vic" went to a party alone.

At some unspecified point, Lydia came to believe that her husband had a zipper problem. Convinced of Louis's infidelity, Lydia tailed him around town and even hired three different private investigators to shadow his every movement. When she feared that her paid eyes and ears had filed false reports, she began to follow them.

Lydia always wore a maroon knit cap when undergoing surveillance and once joked to a friend that the hat formed part of her disguise. It was the same hat found a few feet away from her body.

Lydia's suspicions reached a zenith on March 31 when she spotted Louis with Mary Maher, a married thirty-three-year-old typist and sometime model, at the Capitol Cafe on Six Mile. According to Thompson, he and a friend went to a birthday party at Maher's residence that afternoon. Afterward, they took Maher and her girlfriend to the Capitol Cafe.

Lydia appeared on the scene and, upon seeing her husband with the stunning redhead, confronted her. "So you're the woman who is going around with my husband," she shouted. Maher later recalled the painful climax of the confrontation, when Lydia threw acid at her and her girlfriend: "The next thing I remember was an arm flashing past my face; a scream was followed by a terrible ache in my legs, and the odor of burning flesh and

The posh postmodern Thompson residence on Orchard Lake as it appeared at the time of Lydia Thompson's murder in 1945. *Walter P. Reuther Library, Archives of Labor and Urban Affairs, Wayne State University.*

clothing." Both women sustained minor injuries. Thompson paid a $300 settlement to the two women.

By late April, "Vic" apparently had decided to call a time of death on his marriage. Under the date of April 19, Lydia wrote in her diary,

> *Vic got up in the morning, packed his suitcase and at 12 o'clock noon he went away alone, to the north, and left me alone in this colossal home, where there is not one soul, and there is nobody I can say a word to. My God, what a cruel man he is! I never thought that he has no heart. He kissed me goodby [sic] six times, and he drove away. He wants a divorce, and for me it would be more pleasant if I died. Oh God, give him understanding and bring him back to me.*

Vic returned, but according to Lydia's diary, his carousing worsened; he went out for long stretches at a time only to return at all hours of the night, inebriated. The tighter Lydia tried to hold on, the more he slipped from her grasp. They barely talked. In an entry dated April 29, Lydia described their relationship as two ships passing in the night. "He doesn't look at me. He doesn't want to speak with me, and he doesn't even want to call me by my name."

Things continued to go south for Lydia. While Vic supposedly partied, she cried herself to sleep, and when that didn't work, she dulled her anxiety with sleeping pills.

"God knows where he is and what he is doing," she wrote. "It is impossible to describe how it is difficult to live through such an unexpected change in him....I can't believe that a man having lived 22 and a half years with a wife, and in his forty-eighth year, would start to run after all kinds of women. It is very hard for me to live through it, because all these years I was faithful, loving, and hardworking wife."

In the entry dated May 5, she described tailing her husband to a bar off Six Mile. She waited in the parking lot until he emerged with "two prostitutes." She followed them into an apartment, where she found Vic in bed with one of the women. "He was drunk," she wrote. "I excused myself that I had disturbed their pleasure and then we left together, Vic and I, to go to the garage."

They had a reconciliation of sorts in mid-May, when Vic took Lydia out to dinner. "Vic was very kind to me. We spent splendid night at home," Lydia wrote. The next day, Vic dashed any hopes that Lydia harbored for a new start when he packed a bag and left for Miami. Lydia described that fateful moment. "Everything in this world has died for me. Vic pulled out my heart and took it with him. Oh God, give me happiness. Return him to me. End my suffering. Send me death quickly."

On the way, he called Lydia from Atlanta but hung up on her when she expressed a desire to take a flight and join him in Florida. Eight days later, he called from his Miami motel. During the conversation, he let it slip that Helen Budnick was also in Miami.

Lydia's worst fears materialized in the person of Helen Budnick, Thompson's tall, attractive onetime secretary. A little younger (thirty-eight to Lydia's forty-seven), a little prettier and a lot less possessive, Budnick perhaps personified Lydia Thompson's deep insecurities about aging.

Panic-stricken and now certain that Budnick did far more than bookkeeping, Lydia hired a private detective in Florida to find her husband. Meanwhile, she boarded a train out of Detroit. She and her detective traced Thompson to a hotel, where he and Helen Budnick had adjoining rooms.

"As my spies had [a] room just opposite, they were able to hear what was going on in their room," Lydia explained in a subsequent diary entry. "They drank whisky, played cards and later on Vic asked her, 'What are you doing?' she answered him this way, 'I get ready for strip tease dance,' which was found out to be a bitter truth." She found out the "bitter truth" the hard way when she and her detective barged into the room at 3:15 a.m. and apparently found Vic and Helen in flagrante delicto.

According to Budnick, Lydia Thompson became despondent. She downed a handful of sleeping pills with a pint of whiskey chaser. She also tried to jump from the sixth story of the hotel, but Thompson talked her off the ledge. The three corners of the love triangle talked throughout the morning, and Helen agreed to stay away from Vic for a period of three months. Vic then drove Lydia back to Orchard Lake. By this point, the Thompson marriage had devolved into nothing more than a marriage certificate bearing their names. And now, to Lydia's horror, Thompson apparently wanted to tear up the document, she believed, because he wanted to replace her with the pretty office staffer.

In one of the last entries, Lydia wrote, "He wants a divorce, but for me it would be more pleasant if I died."

The diary, which abruptly ended on June 20, told the tragic story of a woman who just could not say goodbye to her allegedly philandering husband, a woman who realized that she had lost her man to a younger, prettier rival and who repeatedly expressed a death wish. The entries in Lydia's calendar depicted Vic as a womanizing cad with an overactive libido, but her constant surveillance of both her husband and her "spies" suggests a paranoia that raises some doubts about the accuracy of the entries. She seems to have had a pattern of jumping to conclusions whenever she saw her husband talking to another woman, particularly if that woman—like Mary Maher—was young and attractive.

Helen Budnick, the supposed homewrecker and office siren, offered a different version of events when detectives grilled the alleged lovebirds on Monday, October 15, in Pontiac. She insisted her relationship with Thompson had at first been platonic and characterized her former boss as a stalker who would not take "no" for an answer. She repeatedly resisted his unwanted advances. Fed up, she quit her job and ran away to Florida, but Thompson followed her and even checked into the same hotel—the hotel in which Lydia Thompson, according to one diary entry, caught them in a compromising position. Eventually, Budnick admitted that her two-year-long "intimate" friendship with Vic caused the breakup of the Thompson marriage.

After the Florida incident, Budnick returned to Detroit, but neither of the Thompsons, she said, would leave her alone. Smitten, Mr. Thompson just could not stay away. "You've got a loyal wife, a good wife," Budnick pleaded with the lovesick man. "Why don't you go home to her?"

Mrs. Thompson also dropped in on the other woman and begged her to stop seeing her husband. Budnick said that Vic's constant appearances on her doorstep made that a near impossibility. In an attempt to assuage the distraught woman, Budnick insisted that she did not love Thompson and hoped to reconcile with her estranged husband.

By July, the Thompson marriage had all but officially ended, and they separated. Lydia stayed at Orchard Lake, and Vic moved into the apartment above the laundry.

On Friday, October 12, Thompson dropped by the house, he said, because Lydia had asked him to check on a water softener. When he arrived, he found the door locked, so he returned to the apartment. That night he went to a party with Helen.

Thompson could think of no reason why anyone might want to harm Lydia. When asked if his wife might have had somebody on the side, Thompson said, "A more pure woman never lived." He also discounted the possibility of theft because Lydia did not carry large sums of money, and he led detectives to a $3,000 cache of diamonds and rubies that they had overlooked during an earlier search of the Orchard Lake property. Thieves would not have overlooked the jewelry.

Although both Budnick and Thompson had airtight alibis for the night of Lydia's murder, the police still viewed them as prime suspects. Thompson's demeanor upon learning of his wife's violent end raised more than a few eyebrows. He did not appear the least bit distraught. When he viewed her nearly decapitated corpse on the slab at the undertaker's, he simply noted, "That's her," without a hint of emotion in his voice. The press made much of his response to viewing a crime scene photo of Lydia's almost-decollated corpse: "Poor kid," he muttered.

And then there was Lydia's tell-all calendar diary. Some detectives saw in Helen Budnick a motive personified and became blind to all other possibilities except one: the husband must have done it. Indeed, years later, investigators faced criticism for their one-dimensional treatment of the case. Some even whispered that while detectives focused their probe on Thompson, other promising leads evaporated.

The prime suspects had convincing alibis. Annabelle Wey, who operated a roadhouse in Macomb County, said that Vic Thompson and Helen Budnick spent the evening of Thursday, October 11, in her establishment. Also present in the roadhouse that evening, Mount Clemens police chief Arthur Rosso supported the alibi. According to Wey, Vic Thompson remained at the roadhouse from Friday evening until Sunday morning, when his wife's body was discovered.

Both Thompson and Budnick, who could feel which way the wind was blowing downtown, requested lie detector tests to prove their innocence. On Tuesday, October 16, investigators took them to State Police Headquarters in East Lansing for the polygraphs.

Helen Budnick appeared nervous after her seventy-five-minute test and at one point remarked, "I'm very upset." The two-and-a-half-hour inquisition apparently did not faze Thompson, whose ear-to-ear smile suggested his satisfaction with the outcome.

State police captain Harold Mulbar seemed less satisfied. He summarized the test results in a statement released later that day. "Sufficient evidence is not shown from the examinations to indicate guilt of either subject," he said, "and the tests did not show that either one had knowledge of the crime."

However, Mulbar suspected that Thompson held back some information. "There were disturbing elements shown in the tests in the case of Thompson. These disturbing factors were no admission of criminal offense. In some cases he hadn't told officers everything."

One of the officers who escorted the pair from Pontiac overhead a snippet of conversation that suggested Budnick did not entirely believe Thompson, either. "If you did this why don't you tell them?" she asked. "Look at the spot I'm in."

"For Heaven's sake, stop it!" Thompson replied. "I did not do it."

Oakland County sheriff Edward K. Thomas believed him. Thomas told reporters that he believed neither Budnick nor Thompson had a hand in the crime.

After the tests, Helen went free, but Thompson remained in custody while detectives checked and rechecked every detail of his alibi. Finally convinced that Vic had nothing to do with his wife's murder, they released him five days later.

Thousands of morbidly curious onlookers attempted to catch a glimpse of Lydia Thompson, lying in state at the Salowich Funeral Home. Keenly

Mourners at Lydia Thompson's Russian Orthodox funeral. Louis V. Thompson, holding a candle, stands second from the left. *Walter P. Reuther Library, Archives of Labor and Urban Affairs, Wayne State University.*

aware that the killer or killers might stand among them, spectators—most of them armchair detectives who never met the departed—cast furtive glances at one another and eyed each other suspiciously.

A *Detroit Times* reporter described the gapers' block. "Thousands of solemnly curious persons paraded over the weekend past the bier of Mrs. Lydia Thompson, trying to read in her calm and immutable face the awful secret of her death. These visitors were, for the most part, the same people who are seen everywhere human drama is enacted—the insatiable patrons of police courts, murder trials and public morgues."

In the ensuing days, a cast of shady characters entered and exited the investigation, only further deepening the mystery surrounding Lydia Thompson's murder.

Police managed to locate a "Perrone." Like the "Perrone" mentioned in the note found in the Orchard Lake house, Samuel Perrone owned a gas station on East Jefferson Avenue. An affluent building contractor who lived in Grosse Pointe, Perrone endured a lengthy interrogation and convinced detectives he had no connections whatsoever with Lydia Thompson.

A bizarre tangle involving two barbers and a beautician made the case even more convoluted. In late October, a promising lead emerged when Detroit police received an anonymous note naming two new suspects in the baffling murder inquiry. The writer of the note, Eugene Suragen, a Russian-born employee of a Woodward Avenue barbershop, told an intriguing story. Suragen claimed he overheard shop owner William Jantilo and Marie Dodenhoft, a beautician who rented a space on the premises, make some incriminating statements about the Lydia Thompson murder.

Suragen said that on October 12, he overheard Dodenhoft ask Jantilo, "Did you do a good job? Where are the jewels? Did you get them for me?"

Jantilo responded, "Yes, everything is all taken care of."

Suragen also described an incident that allegedly took place a few days after Lydia Thompson's murder. Jantilo came to the barbershop with a shovel and spent half of the day in the basement, perhaps burying something under the cellar floor. The barber did not waver; he told the same story several times to different detectives.

Dragged into custody, the new suspects underwent several hours of intense grilling. Both denied even knowing Lydia Thompson, but admissions Dodenhoft allegedly made to detectives echoed off the walls of police headquarters and into the ears of eager reporters, ending up as the following day's front-page news. The *Detroit Free Press* proclaimed, in a margin-to-margin headline running across page one of the October 29 edition, "CONFESSION IN AXE DEATH CLAIMED BY CITY POLICE."

While Jantilo and Dodenhoft underwent interrogation, detectives searched for physical evidence linking their new suspects to the crime. They found blood-like speckles on the front seat and gear shift knob of Jantilo's car (which, coincidentally, he had purchased from Vic Thompson's dealership) and hit pay dirt when they unearthed a rusty .32 revolver and $200 in cash under the cellar floor. It all seemed too pat to Oakland County sheriff Edward K. Thomas, who said the barbershop angle "smelled."

What at first appeared to bring closure to a vexing murder mystery turned out to be just another dead end. Forensic scientists could not establish if the "blood spatter" was in fact human blood, and they could not lift a fingerprint from the revolver, which hadn't been fired in years. Jantilo also passed a polygraph that indicated he knew nothing about the crime. After five days of relentless interrogation, authorities released the barber and the beautician.

Upon his release, William Jantilo leveled an accusation of his own: Detroit police, he said, used the third degree; they manhandled him, repeatedly punching him and slamming his head against the walls.

Eugene Suragen also reportedly took a lie detector test, but the state police did not release the results. When a reporter asked Captain Leonard if the release of Jantilo and Dodenhoft meant they did not believe Suragen, Leonard quipped, "Well, we released them didn't we?"

Curiously, according to an employee of the Thompson laundry business, where Lydia spent her days working, William Jantilo was a regular customer.

At about the same time as the barbershop angle broke, the police released the interpreter's translation of Lydia Thompson's so-called diary, perhaps in the hope that it would churn up new leads. Both the *Detroit Free Press* and the *Detroit Times* ran front-page stories containing the transcript. The salacious entries that documented allegations of adultery and prostitution made fascinating reading, and newsstands quickly sold out of papers.

Another curious character materialized in the form of an aged Russian immigrant named Andrew Shevchenko, Lydia Thompson's father. The seventy-year-old, who did not speak English, contacted authorities through a local couple and said that he wanted to see his daughter's body. Shevchenko became a person of interest when police found a note, ostensibly penned by Lydia Thompson, bequeathing all of her worldly property to him. Lydia also left her father a note, in Russian, in which she provided a postmortem clue: if anything happened to her, the note indicated, Shevchenko should find a certain individual "on Jefferson."

Shevchenko was a gourmet chef specializing in Russian cuisine, reportedly the best of his kind in Detroit, but instead of making borscht, he pushed a mop at a local church. He had moved to America twenty-two years earlier, spending all but the most recent three months in New York, yet he did not speak a word of English and did all of his communicating with the police through translators.

Shevchenko arrived in Detroit on July 27, he said, at Lydia's request. He had not seen her in decades, the last time being before she married her first husband in Russia. She set him up in an apartment, where she visited him several times a week. She appeared nervous and frequently burst into tears, but despite his prodding, she would not tell him about the cause of her distress.

Lydia Thompson apparently did not tell anybody about her father's presence in the Motor City, even her husband. This peculiar scenario, which detectives characterized as a "backstreet relationship," raised more than a few eyebrows.

In outlining the prominent characters in the case, *Detroit Times* writer Elmer Williams mentioned a provocative tidbit: "Among his daughter's [Lydia's] possessions is a picture of her father, carrying an ax."

Some speculation arose as to whether Shevchenko was Lydia Thompson's real father. He went to the funeral, knelt by the side of the coffin, appeared distressed at her passing and answered—through a translator—police inquiries. Yet he spoke no English, which raised some suspicions about the true history of his emigration.

After intense grilling, which included truth serum (both Shevchenko and Vic Thompson submitted to sodium pentothal at the University of Michigan Hospital), he walked out of the police station as a free man and promised not to leave town without notifying authorities.

He did not keep his part of the bargain. As the barber and the beautician left police custody, Shevchenko re-entered it; police arrested him when he tried to skip town, he said, to take a chef's job in the north.

After verifying that Shevchenko was in fact Lydia Andreyevna's father, detectives questioned him about his "backstreet relationship" with Lydia but once again reached a dead end and let him go.

Frustrated with a lack of progress in the case and facing immense pressure to solve one of the most brutal murders in Oakland County history, top brass formed a multi-jurisdictional team of detectives. The all-star squad of investigators, heralded as the first of its kind in Michigan history and designed to avoid intra-department feuds, planned on questioning anyone and everyone associated with the Thompsons in the hope of finding new clues.

Over the weeks and months after Lydia Thompson's murder, clues continued to surface occasionally. A second examination of her car by State Police revealed traces of blood. The finding came amid criticism that detectives bungled the first search and obliterated any fingerprints left in the vehicle.

One particular clue created a great deal of head-scratching downtown. A friend and former neighbor of Helen Budnick who was helping Vic Thompson clean the Orchard Lake house discovered Lydia's purse stashed under the kitchen refrigerator. He gave the purse to Vic, who immediately called police. Vic also found Lydia's handgun cached behind a panel in a closet. Those involved in the original search of the residence swore that they had looked in every nook and cranny, including under the refrigerator, but found nothing.

Detectives heard whispers from the Detroit underworld that Lydia had at one time hired two thugs to rough up Vic's many lady friends, although the lead would remain apocryphal.

In 1946, Oakland County authorities received an enigmatic telegram from Russia, supposedly from Lydia Thompson's sister. According to the sender, Lydia Thompson's father had died years earlier in Russia.

Another fascinating clue involved Lydia's bequest. A comparison of the handwriting on the note, which left all of Lydia's possessions to her father, to the handwriting on Lydia's calendar-diary revealed that the penmanship did not match. The handwriting analysis raised an interesting question about the note's authenticity.

In February 1946—four months after the savage murder—Helen Budnick became the second Mrs. Thompson. The couple moved into the postmodern mansion nestled along the edge of Orchard Lake, but little did the newlyweds suspect that detectives would interrupt their happily-ever-after in March 1947.

The case stalled in Oakland County, so Wayne County prosecutors revamped the investigation, basing their new and renewed efforts on the supposition that Lydia Thompson's murder occurred in Wayne rather than Oakland

County, which gave them jurisdiction. A year after the discovery of Lydia Thompson's body, a grand jury convened. Several times over the ensuing weeks, Vic and Helen Thompson went to the National Bank Building, where the grand jury met, and answered questions.

In March 1947, the grand jury issued a warrant charging the couple for the murder of Lydia Thompson along with "John Doe," "Richard Roe" and "Mary Roe." On the pretext of answering yet more questions for the grand jury, they agreed to accompany detectives to Detroit, where they were arrested and lodged in the county jail. The arrests came as no surprise to the couple. Helen Thompson remarked that she had "expected it," characterizing the new ordeal as the darkness before the dawn. Both she and Vic expressed their hopes that this new round of scrutiny would clear them for good.

A few days later, investigators arrested one of the pseudonymous, alleged coconspirators: Stanley Anculewicz, a thirty-three-year-old ex-convict involved in an extramarital tryst with a married woman named Laura Riddle.

According to Riddle, Anculewicz bragged about his role as the heavy in a murder-for-hire conspiracy to do away with Lydia Thompson. Louis

Mrs. Louis V. Thompson—Helen Budnick—in 1947. *Walter P. Reuther Library, Archives of Labor and Urban Affairs, Wayne State University.*

Louis V. Thompson after his arrest in 1947. *Walter P. Reuther Library, Archives of Labor and Urban Affairs, Wayne State University.*

Thompson is fingerprinted following his arrest in 1947. *Walter P. Reuther Library, Archives of Labor and Urban Affairs, Wayne State University.*

Thompson, Anculewicz told Riddle, paid him $10,000 to murder his meddlesome first wife to make way for Helen Budnick.

Confronted with his own loose lips, Anculewicz admitted telling the tale but claimed that he had fabricated the entire story to get rid of Riddle, who wanted him to leave his wife. She might have second thoughts, he reasoned, about a long-term relationship with a killer. Anculewicz had a reputation as a tall-tale teller. Even Riddle characterized him as "an awful liar."

Anculewicz returned the sentiment when he spoke to a reporter from behind bars.

"I've been telling her some pretty good lies," Anculewicz said during the brief interview, "but my lies are all right because I admit them later. Now you take her lies. Hers are bad because she's all mixed up in them."

When the grand jury learned that Riddle might have obtained some details about the murder from discussions with a reporter, the case against

Anculewicz evaporated. The indictment was dismissed, and he walked out of jail a free man in mid-April.

Although the specter of a possible trial lingered until May, the case atrophied when prosecutors failed to show that Lydia Thompson died in Wayne County. Vic and Helen left custody and reportedly took a vacation in Bermuda. Their ordeal had finally ended, and the case grew cold. In the eighty years since the discovery of Lydia Thompson's body on the side of a lonely road in Oakland County, investigators have come no closer to solving the bizarre crime.

During the fall of 1945, the Lydia Thompson case became a popular subject among armchair detectives. They posited theories and debated where the clues did or did not fit.

One provocative theory, proposed by Vic Thompson and forwarded by the *Detroit News* in a page-one item of October 30, 1945, had Lydia Thompson plotting the murder-suicide of her and her husband. Since she lacked the fortitude to do the dirty work herself, she hired a hit man to carry out the ultimate "if I can't have him no one will" scenario. Helen Budnick believed that her name was also on the hit list.

Thompson believed that Lydia dropped not-so-subtle hints of her murder-suicide plot. According to Lydia's closest friend and confidante Harriet Steele, Lydia once remarked, "When Vic dies, I die too." At another time, she told Steele, "I will kill Vic and Helen and myself" and repeated the threat in front of Vic during another visit with Steele. At the time, both Thompson and Steele did not take the threats seriously and thought Lydia was joking.

Lydia's finances also tended to support Vic's conspiracy theory. In the weeks before her death, she borrowed $1,000 from a friend, supposedly to set up her father in business. She also retrieved approximately $3,000 in war bonds that Steele held for her. Perhaps the money went for a cause other than Shevchenko. When police grilled Shevchenko in Pontiac, the old man denied ever receiving the money from Lydia.

Thompson outlined what he believed happened just after dusk on October 11. That afternoon, Lydia drove to Detroit, where she met the hired assassin or assassins. Because she did not like to drive at night, she left her car in Detroit while the hit man drove her home to Orchard Lake.

After dark, they left Orchard Lake, possibly on the pretext of watching the murder of her husband, but the plot went awry when something set her off, possibly the killer's reluctance to follow through, which led to a violent and ultimately fatal confrontation. Or the killer never intended to murder Vic and Helen, only to take Lydia's money and silence the witness. Or the killer's or killers' nerves failed after carrying out one of the murders—that of Lydia Thompson. After Lydia's death, her killer or killers dumped the body and then parked her car in a Pontiac parking lot.

The image of a willing, perhaps even eager, Lydia Thompson leaving her Orchard Lake mansion with a hit man to witness the murder of her husband, however, does not fit the reality of a near-frantic Lydia Thompson, terrified for her life, on the afternoon of October 11. It also doesn't jive with the antemortem wounds running the length of Lydia Thompson's torso.

A more likely cognate to Vic Thompson's murder-suicide theory: at some point, Lydia may have had cold feet and decided to cancel the contract, except she did not know how to reach the operatives. Desperate, she went to the grocery store owner for help in finding the man whose name she carried on a small slip of paper. Failing in this attempt, her desperation turned into panic. By the time she met with Steele, she had become frantic. She referenced the handgun she had acquired and intimated that the slip of paper meant life or death.

The gun, which Lydia would have acquired to protect herself from a fate she herself had arranged, was the biggest hole in Vic's theory. According to local cops, Lydia came to the station several months before October 11 and expressed an urgent need for a handgun. She also told Harriet Steele she planned to buy a gun. Canceling the contract at the eleventh hour would not explain why she felt a need for a weapon months earlier.

Another possibility that made the rounds among armchair detectives: Lydia committed suicide by proxy in order to frame Vic and thus prevent him from a happily-ever-after with Helen Budnick. This theory would explain the damning diary entries, which described Vic's alleged infidelities in graphic detail, and the obvious place Lydia left it—not buried under lingerie in her underwear drawer but prominently positioned where detectives were sure to find it. This theory, however, fails the litmus test of logic. Would Lydia Thompson have submitted to torture with a hot icepick and a brutally violent demise to avenge her husband's affair with another woman?

Lydia Thompson, some believed, fell victim to a wandering psychopath. In the earliest phase of the investigation, detectives from Windsor came to Detroit to view the body because they suspected that she might have been another victim in a string of murders there. They left convinced that the cases were not linked, but Lydia's concern about a "prowler" hanging around the Orchard Lake home—a worry significant enough to warrant acquiring a gun—tends to suggest more of a random attack than a murder conspiracy. The two-month time lapse between that incident and the murder, however, tends to undermine the wandering psychopath theory.

In the week after Lydia Thompson's murder, Vic Thompson and the *Detroit News* each offered a $1,000 reward for information leading to the arrest of the parties responsible for the crime. Those rewards were never claimed, and the case remains one of the most baffling unsolved crimes in Michigan history.

9

The Four

(Lansing, 1970-1972)

In the early seventies, the murder of four women shocked Lansing residents, startled coeds and confounded investigators. It is a saga of frustrating dead ends and unanswered questions but also an exemplar of how modern science can thaw very old, very cold cases.

Nineteen-year-old Michigan State University coed Diane Osinski looked like the girl next door. The most widely circulating photograph shows a teenager with long, brown stick-straight hair parted neatly down the middle, accentuating her oval face. A broad, toothy smile reveals a capped incisor.

Osinski, a native of Hamtramck, studied psychology and lived in a single room in an off-campus house. At about 11:00 a.m. on the morning of July 24, 1972, she left her apartment shortly after receiving a telephone call from a man who supposedly offered her an interview for a babysitting job. This was the second call from the client, the first coming through about ninety minutes earlier. Apparently, there was a misunderstanding about the meeting time. "Oh, I'm sorry, I didn't mean to keep you waiting," Diane said during the second call. "I thought you meant 10:30 tonight." She told her housemates about the appointment, grabbed her purse and left. She never returned.

Two days later, police learned of Osinski's disappearance and began a search. A missing coed was not a new scenario to East Lansing police. College kids fell in love, fell out of love, cohabitated, spent long weekends together, eloped or just plain ran away. Usually, they packed a bag. Diane Osinski did not. If she decided to leave for some reason—a scenario that seemed out of character for the atypically grounded student—she left without taking her prescription eyeglasses, checkbook, bank book, a change of clothes or toiletries. She had not touched her checking account; the balance remained at the same level—one hundred dollars—as before her disappearance.

Besides, Diane had no reason to run away. By all accounts, she had a healthy relationship with her family in Hamtramck. All of the clues pointed to Diane as the victim of foul play. In an attempt to churn up new leads and possible eyewitnesses who saw Diane on the day she disappeared, police circulated a description of their missing person: five-foot, four-inch, 110-pound female with light-brown hair and blue eyes wearing dark-colored jeans, sandals and a blouse.

To residents of East Lansing, the Osinski disappearance must have felt like déjà vu. When a week passed with no sign of the missing coed, locals began to worry that history was about to repeat itself.

On Saturday, November 21, 1970, a body turned up in a wooded "lovers' lane" on the southern fringe of Michigan State University's campus. The remote location, which made it ideal for clandestine assignations, also made it ideal for concealing a body. Nude except for a brassiere wrapped loosely around her neck and a pair of tennis shoes, the body was located in a copse of white pine about fifty yards from a dirt two-track road. The absence of clothes on the body hinted at a lovers' tryst somehow gone tragically wrong.

By tracing a high school class ring on the body, police identified the young woman as eighteen-year-old Marie Ann Jackson, an attractive brunette with shoulder-length hair. A postmortem revealed that Marie Ann Jackson's killer had raped and strangled her with some type of ligature such as a cord.

The best guess had Jackson's murder occurring sometime around a week before the discovery of her body. Jackson worked as a waitress at a local drive-through restaurant but had not reported for work since November 13. That evening, Jackson was seen at a local fast-food restaurant on Cedar

Street in an old, beat-up Oldsmobile convertible with a man described as a male in his thirties.

A second sighting put Jackson in another car the night before the discovery of her body. As the investigation progressed, a witness came forward and told of seeing Jackson as a passenger riding in a souped-up Chevrolet Impala on Friday, November 20. Jackson enjoyed hitchhiking and bummed rides around the city, so these sightings may have been nothing more than an adventurous teenager's mode of transportation.

In the ensuing investigation, a half-dozen suspects emerged, including Carl Fitch, a twenty-three-year-old resident of nearby Eaton Rapids. Fitch adamantly denied any involvement in the murder, and without a scintilla of evidence placing him at the scene, the case against him fizzled. Likewise for the other suspects.

The investigation was still ongoing when, eighteen months after the discovery of Marie Ann Jackson's body, Dianne Osinski dropped out of sight.

The key to finding Diane Osinski, it appeared, was in finding the mysterious caller who had offered her a babysitting job. This lead turned into a frustrating dead end.

Investigators learned that Diane worked at a local daycare center, apparently liked the work and subsequently applied for babysitting postings through the university's student placement service. Through this avenue, Diane's contact information was given to several potential clients, but the service did not record the names or contact information of those people, which effectively meant that investigators had reached an impasse in tracing the as-yet-unidentified caller.

Investigators still had not managed to identify Osinski's caller when two more women died violent deaths at the hands of unknown assailants within eight days in August 1972.

The body of forty-three-year-old Betty Jean Goodrich, last seen in the parking lot of a grocery store on August 11, 1972, turned up in a densely wooded area in the rural village of Nashville, a little over forty miles east of Lansing. She was stabbed in the chest four times with an edged weapon and garroted with her own belt. Except for the sketchy report of a shopper who remembered seeing Goodrich in the parking lot earlier that day, no one had seen anything.

Charles Joseph Emery, an ex-convict on parole, became a prime suspect in the Goodrich slaying. In 1958, Emery, masquerading as an interested homebuyer, talked his way into a house in Jackson, kidnapped the occupant, drove her to a game area thirteen miles east of the city and "criminally assaulted" her. He then dropped her off three blocks from her home. She survived and provided police with the license plate number, which led to Emery and subsequent convictions for kidnapping and rape. He was sentenced to thirty to sixty years but released early on parole. The parallels to the Goodrich case were evident, but there wasn't enough evidence to warrant a charge.

A little over a week after the Goodrich murder, on August 19, fifty-eight-year-old Irene Waters left her apartment, apparently after receiving a bogus phone call notifying her that her place of employment—a doctor's office—had burst into flames. An unidentified assailant attacked her after she went into the garage, stabbing her fifteen times. As Waters lay dying, the man darted down an adjacent alley. A witness later described the man, which led to a composite sketch.

As winter approached and the temperatures dropped, the investigations into all three cases had cooled. Investigators exhausted all leads in the Osinski disappearance, and hopes of finding her alive had fallen with the leaves.

Diane's twentieth birthday—December 15—came and went without the birthday girl making an appearance. By the end of 1972, hopes of finding Diane Osinski alive and well had faded into the reality that the missing persons case had now become a search for yet another body dumped in a remote location somewhere on the edge of the city.

Diane's grandmother understood this reality. "I believed from the first day she was dead," Katherine Mroz said during an interview with the press in late November. "But they've been finding girls. Finding girls. I've been watching the news. Here. Here. But not her."

Ten months after Diane Osinski dropped out of sight, her skeleton turned up in a wooded conservation area in Bath Township about ten miles north of East Lansing. Clothes on the skeleton matched those worn by Osinski when she rushed out of her apartment to meet a potential employer, and a dental comparison clinched the identification. A forensic examination failed to uncover a cause of death.

The elements had done considerable damage to Osinski's skeleton. Scavenging animals had made off with some of the bones and a ring Diane was wearing on the day of her disappearance.

The densely forested area had apparently been used as a trysting spot for MSU students, who left the telltale detritus commonly associated with lovers' lane activity: used condoms, empty beer cans and soiled underwear. According to an item in the *Lansing State Journal*, police at one time busted a group filming "a sex orgy" in the vicinity where Osinski's skeleton surfaced.

Discovery and positive identification of the skeleton led to more questions than answers. Diane Osinski was no longer missing, but what had happened to her remained nothing but question marks.

In 1982, Texas authorities arrested serial killer Coral Watts, the "Sunday Morning Slasher," who allegedly murdered a string of coeds in Ann Arbor in the mid-seventies. The Inkster native fled Michigan when investigators identified him as a person of interest. While in Houston, Texas, Watts was captured during an attempted double homicide. He subsequently cut a deal with prosecutors. In exchange for a sixty-year prison sentence, he copped to about a dozen murders in Texas.

Although Watts's serial crimes supposedly begin in 1974, his preferred use of edged weapons and his choice of victims made him a potential suspect in several unsolved Michigan murders, including the slayings of Goodrich and Waters and presumed murder of Diane Osinski.

When a technicality nearly led to Watts's release, Michigan authorities moved to extradite him. Tried, convicted and sentenced to life (and subsequently given a second life sentence after a second conviction), Watts died in prison of prostate cancer in 2007. If he had a hand in any of the Lansing cases, he never said.

Watts committed murders in several jurisdictions in at least two states, but did the "Sunday Morning Slasher" also stalk women in Lansing? Without a cause of death, there was too little to suggest Watts had a hand in Diane Osinski's demise. And since Watts did not rape or sexually molest his victims, he seemed a poor fit for "Mr. X" in the Marie Anne Jackson case.

Goodrich and Waters, however, were both stabbed multiple times, so when Watts's arrest in Texas made national headlines in 1982, he became a topic of conversation in Lansing. While Watts seemed like a longshot (he was eighteen years old in 1972 and investigators had already identified a prime suspect in the Goodrich slaying), he couldn't be entirely dismissed, either.

Under the microscope, however, Watts was an unlikely suspect in either the Osinski or the Waters case. If an unknown voice on the other end of a telephone line lured Osinski with the possibility of a babysitting job, and an unknown voice likewise lured Irene Waters from her apartment with a phony story about a burning office building, then this parallel—either a chilling coincidence or a link connecting the two cases—tends to discount Coral Watts as a viable suspect. During his string of murders, he typically chose victims at random and attacked swiftly and without warning.

The advent of DNA testing led to significant epilogues in two of the four cases. In 2001, a DNA test linked Charles Joseph Emery to the murder of Betty Ann Goodrich. Emery, who emerged as a suspect during the original investigation, died in 1992, which leaves the case without the legal closure of a trial.

Closure in the Marie Anne Jackson case came thirty-eight years later when DNA testing provided the missing link between Jackson and Carl Finch, an original suspect in the case. After Finch committed suicide in Florida in 1997, DNA in a tissue sample taken from his body matched DNA in body fluid recovered from the crime scene in 1970. Investigators suspected Finch at the time but didn't have enough evidence to charge him.

The Irene Waters and Diane Osinski cases remain unsolved mysteries.

For Additional Research

1. The "Spiked Club Triple Murder" (Dowagiac, 1921)

Detroit Free Press. September 21–29, 1921.

Dowagiac Daily News. September 21–29, 1921.

Goll, Ralph, and Donald F. Schram. "The Strange Case of the 3 Bold Murders and Midnight." *Detroit Free Press*, February 28, 1943.

Herald-Press (St. Joseph, MI). September 21–29, 1921; November 28–December 10, 1921.

News-Palladium (Benton Harbor, MI). September 21–29, 1921.

South Bend (IN) News Times. September 21–29, 1921.

South Bend (IN) Tribune, September 21—28, 1921

2. The Ferndale Head Case (Ferndale, 1927)

Chicago Tribune. February 14, 1927.

Daily Clarion-Ledger (Jackson, MI). January 17, 1935; March 6, 1935.

Detroit Free Press. February 13–17, 1927.

Detroit Times. February 12–17, 1927; January 15, 1935; February 5, 1935.

Goll, Ralph, and Donald F. Schram. "The Strange Case of the 4 Heads without a Single Body." *Detroit Free Press*, January 24, 1943.

Indianapolis Star. February 14, 1927.

Lake County Times (Hammond, IN). October 5, 1926.

Muncie (IN) Evening Press. February 16, 1927.

The Muncie (IN) Morning Star. February 14, 1927.

3. The Doctor, His Wife and the Other Woman (Detroit, 1927)

Detroit Free Press. February 24–March 1, 1927; April 1–27, 1927; May 22–June 8, 1927; May 19–26, 1928.
Detroit Times. February 23–March 1, 1927; April 13–27, 1927; May 24–June 10, 1927; May 19–26, 1928.
Givens, Charles. "Murder Domestic: The Loomis Case." In *Detroit Murders*, edited by Alvin C. Hamer, 61–88. New York: Duell, Sloan and Pearce, 1948.
Levins, Peter. "Fear on Every Side." *Detroit Times*, March 31, 1946.
———. "Their Killers Went Free!" *Detroit Free Press*, April 21, 1940.
Oates, Morgan. "What Goes On Here: Was This Picture Key to the Loomis Murder?" *Detroit Free Press*, November 23, 1958.
Smits, Lee J. "Mrs. Loomis' Slayer Allowed to Escape as Victims' Screams Go Unheeded." *Detroit Sunday Times*, November 11, 1934.

4. The St. Aubin Avenue House of Horrors (Detroit, 1929)

Crowley, James G. "Detroit's Strange Cults—Evangelista Murder." *Detroit Evening Times*, May 29, 1936.
Detroit Free Press. July 4–16, 1929; August 18, 20, 30, 1935.
Detroit Times. July 4–16, 1929; June 30, 1930.
———. "The Six Evangelista Ax Murders." June 1, 1938.
Howes, Royce. "Six Killings and a Cult: The Evangelista Case." In *Detroit Murders*, edited by Alvin C. Hamer, 91–115. New York: Duell, Sloan and Pearce, 1948.

5. He Talked Too Much : Jerry Buckley (Detroit, 1930)

Detroit Free Press. July 23–31, 1930.
Detroit Times. July 23–30, 1930.
Haun, Charles T. "Bloody July: The Buckley Case." In *Detroit Murders*, edited by Alvin C. Hamer, 119–34. New York: Duell, Sloan and Pearce, 1948.
Murray, Riley. "Who Killed Jerry Buckley?" *Detroit Free Press*, July 17, 1955.
Shermerhorn, Jack, and George A. Hough III. "Lobby Death: Crusading Jerry Buckley Silenced by Murderers' Bullets." *Detroit Free Press*, September 7, 1947.

6. "A Riddle, Wrapped in a Mystery, inside an Enigma" (Grand Rapids, 1938)

Detroit Free Press, March 28, 1943.

Detroit Times. March 5–8, 1938.

Goll, Ralph, and Donald F. Schram. "The Strange Case of the Murdered Choir Singer."

Grand Rapids Herald. March 4–13, 1938.

Grand Rapids Press. March 4–13, 1938; March 30–31, 1938; March 4, 1948; March 1, 1958; March 22, 1987.

Kaufman, Al. "Unsolved Michigan Crimes: Murder of Pretty Mina Dekker Still a Mystery after More Than Four Years of Investigation." *Detroit Times*, July 12, 1942.

LaMarre, Virgil E. "Murder of the Beautiful Typist." *True Detective Mysteries* 31, no. 2 (November 1938): 34–39; 115–17.

The Mina Dekker Case File, 1938–2020, Grand Rapids Police Department.

Schock, David B., PhD. "Murder on the Third Floor." Delayedjustice.com.

7. The Usual Suspects: The Slaying of Senator Warren Hooper (Lansing, 1945)

Battle Creek Enquirer. May 13–14, 1945; July 20, 1945.

Detroit Free Press. January 12–14, 1945; May 13–15, 1945; July 20, 1945; August 1, 1945.

The Donald S. Leonard Michigan State Police Files, 1932–1954. Bentley Historical Library, the University of Michigan, Ann Arbor, Michigan.

The Donald S. Leonard Papers, 1925–1966. Bentley Historical Library, the University of Michigan, Ann Arbor, Michigan.

Lansing State Journal, January 12–14; May 13–15, 1945; July 20, 1945; August 1, 1945.

8. The Riddle of Lydia Thompson (Detroit, 1945)

Bronte, Patricia. "Strange Woman: The Lydia Thompson Case." In *Detroit Murders*, edited by Alvin C. Hamer, 197–218. New York: Duell, Sloan and Pearce, 1948.

Detroit Free Press. October 15–November 3, 1945; March 23–March 25, 1947.

Detroit Times. October 15–November 3, 1945; March 23–March 25, 1947.

Murray, Riley. "Who Killed Lydia Thompson?" *Detroit Free Press*, October 16, 1955.

9. The Four (Lansing, 1970–1972)

Detroit Free Press. July 22, 1970; August 16, 1972; May 13, 1973.

Lansing State Journal. July 10–21, 1970; November 23, 1970; December 2, 1970; August 16, 21, 27, 1972; November 19, 26, 1972; May 11, 13, 21, 1973; August 24, 1982; August 7, 1983; August 7, 2008; May 27, 2013.

About the Author

A connoisseur of crime, a gourmet of the ghastly, an aficionado of the atrocious, a fanatic of the felonious and a maven of misdeeds, author and researcher Tobin T. Buhk enjoys exploring the back alleys of Michigan history and shining a light on the contemptible characters and dastardly deeds hiding in its darkest corners. *Cold Case Michigan* is his eleventh published book. To research his first book, he spent a year as a volunteer in the Kent County Morgue. Find his speaking schedule at tobinbuhk.com or take a walk on the dark side of history at his blog, darkcornersofhistory.com.

Visit us at
www.historypress.com